AN ARCHAEOLOGY OF UNCHECKED CAPITALISM

An Archaeology of Unchecked Capitalism

From the American Rust Belt to the Developing World

Paul A. Shackel

berghahn
NEW YORK · OXFORD
www.berghahnbooks.com

First published in 2020 by
Berghahn Books
www.berghahnbooks.com

© 2020, 2025 Paul A. Shackel
First paperback edition published in 2025

All rights reserved. Except for the quotation of short passages for the purposes of criticism and review, no part of this book may be reproduced in any form or by any means, electronic or mechanical, including photocopying, recording, or any information storage and retrieval system now known or to be invented, without written permission of the publisher.

Library of Congress Cataloging-in-Publication Data

A C.I.P. cataloging record is available from the Library of Congress
Library of Congress Cataloging in Publication Control Number: 2019041780

British Library Cataloguing in Publication Data

A catalogue record for this book is available from the British Library

EU GPSR Authorized Representative
LOGOS EUROPE, 9 rue Nicolas Poussin, 17000, LA ROCHELLE, France
Email: Contact@logoseurope.eu

ISBN 978-1-78920-547-3 hardback
ISBN 978-1-83695-323-4 paperback
ISBN 978-1-83695-324-1 epub
ISBN 978-1-78920-548-0 web pdf

https://doi.org/10.3167/9781789205473

Some day we will have the courage to rise up and strike back at these great giants of industry, and then we will see that they weren't giants at all. They only seemed so because we were on our knees and they towered over us.
—Mother Jones, 1910

CONTENTS

List of Illustrations and Figures	viii
Acknowledgments	ix
Introduction	1
Chapter 1. The History of Race in the Anthracite Coal Region	12
Chapter 2. An Archaeology of Immigration, Race, and Poverty in the Anthracite Coal Region	29
Chapter 3. Historic Trauma: Health and Well-Being in Northeastern Pennsylvania	50
Chapter 4. Offshoring the Textile Industry and Industrial Tragedy	72
Chapter 5. Offshoring Mining Industries and Tragedy	91
Conclusion. Difficult Histories Are a Reality in the Present	110
References	121
Index	143

ILLUSTRATIONS AND FIGURES

Illustrations

2.1.	Locating the cesspool in the rear of a lot in Pardeesville, Pennsylvania.	47
3.1.	Abandoned mine filled with acid mine drainage.	54
3.2.	Culm bank at Beaver Meadows, Pennsylvania.	70
4.1.	Thousands of garment workers and their unions rally on the first anniversary of the Rana Plaza collapse.	89
5.1.	Police advance after shooting striking workers with live ammunition on 16 August 2012.	95
5.2.	Rescue operation in progress at the Soma mine disaster in Turkey.	103

Figures

1.1.	Location of the anthracite fields in northeastern Pennsylvania.	13
2.1.	Circa 1900 map of Lattimer No. 2.	37
3.1.	Heart disease death rate, 2014–2016, for the white population, ages 35 years and older, by county.	65
3.2.	Coronary heart disease death rates for whites, 35 years and older, 2014–2016, in the anthracite coal region (encircled) of Pennsylvania.	68

ACKNOWLEDGMENTS

The Anthracite Heritage Project has been working in northeastern Pennsylvania since 2009, first detailing the memory and forgetting of one of the most dramatic labor massacres in United States history. Michael Roller coordinated this survey project with Dan Sivilich, President of BRAVO (Battlefield Restoration and Archaeological Volunteer Organization). We are grateful to Pasco Schiavo for allowing us to perform the survey on his property. Later projects explored the social history and heritage of the area. Much of the archaeology described in Chapter 2 was overseen by former graduate students who have since earned their PhDs. They include Michael Roller, V. Camille Westmont, and Justin Uehlein. Local residents Joe Michel, John Probert, and Maurice D'Alessandro were more than willing to share their love for the region's history. As longtime residents of the area, they provided a wealth of material and an entrée into the community. Joe gave us access to "the 110," his collection of documents and maps related to the region. As coal-mining companies closed their operations, they often abandoned their buildings and left behind company records. He salvaged the records of many companies before they were lost to the wrecking ball. He has since donated much of these records to the Historical Collections and Labor Archives (HCLA) at Penn State University Libraries.

Michael Roller supervised the excavations in the Italian village in Lattimer No. 2 (now known as Pardeesville). V. Camille Westmont and Justin Uehlein supervised the excavations at the Yanac house in Lattimer No. 2. Their work is summarized in Chapter 2. More recently, we worked at Eckley Miners' Village, which has become a collaborative program with the Department of Anthropology and the Historic Preservation Program at the University of Maryland. While Eckley is not part of this book, I am indebted to Dr. Bode Morin, Eckley's site administrator. He has provided invaluable experiences for our undergraduates and graduate students. Several years ago he shared with us scientific studies about the general health and well-being of northeastern Pennsylvania, which became an important part of Chapter 3.

Throughout the entire project Angela Fierro, a lifelong resident of Lattimer and owner of the Lattimer company store, was more than generous with her time and resources. She allowed me and my students access to family histories and other primary documents. There are many news reporters working for the local newspaper who brought attention to the project and allowed us to share our story with the community. I am especially grateful to Kent Jackson, who wrote many stories about the Anthracite Heritage Project, emphasizing our program's goal of examining the historical and contemporary issues of work and immigration.

I am grateful to the many reviewers of this manuscript, including Randall McGuire and James Symonds. I also appreciate that Megan Bailey provided helpful comments on the manuscript. The manuscript is a better product because of their helpful input and insights.

INTRODUCTION

For the past decade, I have spent time working on issues related to labor, immigration, and race in the anthracite coal region of northeastern Pennsylvania. The experience has been somewhat transformative for me when I think about how this region is remembered. Descendants often reminisce about getting by, and the official public memory often emphasizes the important role anthracite coal played in the development of the Industrial Revolution. Both perspectives of the past are real. The anthracite coal industry began in the late eighteenth century and developed into a commercial success before the middle of the nineteenth century, and by the turn of the twentieth century, the industry employed about 180,000 workers who extracted over 100 million tons of coal per year. However, generations of new immigrants were subjected to some of the worst working and living conditions in the United States. The extraction of coal came at a huge cost to human lives and had one of the highest occupational mortality rates in the United States. Men were often killed or injured without consequence, and families often lived on the brink of starvation. Some deaths were caused by major tragedies, like the Avondale mine disaster of 1869 (Wolensky and Keating 2008) or the 1959 Knox mine disaster (Wolensky et al. 2005), to name only a few. Other deaths were caused by frequent cave-ins or explosions, maiming and killing a few and sometimes dozens of men at a time. The victims were anonymous, and the tragedies not recognized by the coal company. The workers were seen by the coal operators as interchangeable and easily replaced with unemployed new immigrants. Stronger mining regulations were legislated after the 1869 Avondale mine disaster, although 32,000 men were killed by mining-related accidents in the anthracite region after this date (Richards 2002, 7).

While the region is finding ways to celebrate a heroic past, it must also deal with the long-term impact of environmental degradation related to the coal industry. The anthracite region is the most disturbed rural landscape in Pennsylvania. Diverse hardwood forests filled with wildlife have been replaced with a lunar-like landscape, absent of vegetation, with only unstable, acidic, black shale to punctuate the terrain. While many of the industrial structures, like coal breakers, have vanished from the landscape, culm banks, which are the waste by-products of mining, remain. They can be over one hundred feet high and seen from many miles away (Conlogue 2013). Peter Goin and Elizabeth Raymond (2004, 39) note that the culm banks scattered throughout the landscape are viewed by some of the miners and descendants of the miners as monuments to the hard work performed by numerous annonymous new immigrants who toiled and survived in this dangerous industry. They are a reminder of the inhumane exploitation that former generations endured and survived. These features have become part of the vernacular landscape.

I first became interested in the anthracite region when I read about one of the largest labor massacres in US history in the patch town of Lattimer Mines, near Hazleton, Pennsylvania. As an attempt to control immigration, the Pennsylvania state legislators passed the Campbell Act in 1897, which was supported by the United Mine Workers of America (UMWA). The act stated that coal operators would be taxed three cents a day for each non-US citizen employed in the collieries. The coal operators passed this tax along to their non-naturalized employees. The miners of the Hazleton district, the majority of whom were not naturalized, went on strike, and in doing so challenged the meaning of citizenship and labor practices. Were immigrants and wage workers equal citizens in a democratic republic, or were they a subaltern class subject to the whims and wills of their employers and more advantaged local citizens? The miners went on strike in mid-August 1897. On 10 September, they marched with the American flag, a symbol of both democracy and the protection of their rights under US law. As they approached Lattimer Mines with the goal of closing the colliery, the strikers were gunned down by the sheriff's posse and members of the Coal and Iron Police, and many were shot in their backs as they fled. Nineteen men died at the site as a result of their confrontation with the sheriff and his supporting law enforcement (Novak 1978). What is fascinating to me is that while Lattimer is considered one of the largest labor massacres in US history, it is not part of the national public memory, while other labor tragedies are, such as conflicts at Haymarket, Homestead, and Ludlow (Zinn 2003). Lattimer is not mentioned in any of the major labor history chronicles, and it is not part of the Pennsylvania state curriculum. I became interested in how memory, or in this case, amnesia, could occur and erase the event from our national memory (Shackel 2018a). It also became clear that even when we become more knowledgeable about these past tragic events related to industry, work, and labor, these tragedies still occur, although outside of our national borders and often in developing nations. We are often unaware of the continuation of the exploitation by and horrific consequences of unchecked industrial capitalism in other parts of the world as American industries continue to purchase products created in harsh, exploitative environments. So, that is the challenge set in this book: providing historical and archaeological documentation in a local context (here in the United States), examining the consequences of unchecked capitalism, and then connecting these same issues to contemporary industrial practices in the developing world.

Anthropologists have debated whether practitioners should be advocates for the communities they are studying and researching (Scheper-Hughes 1995) or not (Hastrup and Elsass 1990). There is growing momentum among researchers who believe that scholars do have a responsibility to become involved in a form of advocacy for the oppressed (see, e.g., De León 2012). Historical archaeology, the discipline that uses above- and belowground material culture, ethnography, oral histories, and documentation, may be a vehicle to enlighten and challenge the consequences of unchecked capitalism (McGuire 2008). As Shannon Dawdy (2010, 769) writes, "Historical archaeology has a tenuous epistemological and disciplinary position in the wider field: it uncovers things not yet forgotten. But it could do even more dangerous and productive work . . . by uncovering things thought best forgotten, such as the failures of state projects and the paths of destruction wrought by high capitalism."

While we struggle to remember America's industrial past, it appears as though much of the struggle between labor and capital has been slowly, methodically, and almost completely erased from much of the global north landscapes, with only a few exceptions. Recovering these reminders of labor history is imperative and not only reveals the injustices of the past, but also connects these conditions to the present. If we do make this connection between the past and the present, it becomes clear that many of the exploitive conditions that existed in the past have been exported to similar industries in developing countries. Therefore, this chronicle of the history and conditions of the anthracite region lays the foundation for connecting to contemporary industry and mining circumstances in other parts of the world. Connecting the tragedies of the historic anthracite mining region of northeastern Pennsylvania to the developing world allows us to observe some of the very same conditions industrializing communities face in the twenty-first century. These work conditions have not necessarily changed for the better. In fact, many of the modern labor conditions in the developing world are, to some degree, a reflection of the conditions found in US industry about a century ago (Shackel 2009, 2016).

Heritage work in communities and regions is a vehicle to connect the past with the present and address some of the pressing social justice issues facing contemporary local and global communities. The Lattimer massacre, which occurred in a remote community in northeastern Pennsylvania, seems like an isolated incident with no connection to the present. In reality, it serves as a touchstone, connecting the history and heritage of the anthracite coal miners in northeastern Pennsylvania to the exploited laborers in today's global economy. To make these connections is a powerful vehicle to use heritage to confront inequalities and promote social justice issues as well as to explore history, heritage, and memory making. While the historical records and the archaeological materials provide a framework for the past, it is important to use these examples and think about how our studies in labor are meaningful and related to us today.

If we want to create a socially and economically just present, we need to think critically about how the past is created and challenge the long-held assumption that the past is past. In other words, the past is present, and we need to dismantle the blinders that prevent us from connecting difficult histories to the present (Little and Shackel 2014; Shackel and Roller 2012). For instance, in 1978, Michael Novak of the American Enterprise Institute published a historical novel that focused on the tragedy of the Lattimer massacre. He wrote about the substandard working and living conditions found in the anthracite region of Pennsylvania, as well as the racism toward new immigrants during the late nineteenth century. The *Wall Street Journal* reviewed Novak's book, *The Guns of Lattimer*. The reviewer questioned the value of the novel, saying, "It is tempting to ask Mr. Novak why we really need the book. The incident occurred more than 80 years ago. It sounds like a unique event that would best be forgotten. Besides, American society has changed; American bosses don't act that way toward blue-collar workers anymore" (Wysocki 1978, 24).

It is a common strategy in a system of unchecked capitalism to take tragic episodes in labor history, think of them as lessons of the past, and not consider how inequalities and labor injustices continue to play out in the world today. The reviewer in the *Wall Street Journal* clearly did not want to address the realities of the social consequences of unchecked capitalism. It is important to move out of our comfort zone and connect these historical issues of labor injustice to the present, even when it becomes politically dangerous to do so, as we confront the hidden realities of a global economy (see Shackel 2018a).

An archaeology of unchecked capitalism can be about working with abandoned, ruined places, which allows us to reflect upon the meaning of these places. The remaining rubble is not shapeless, worthless debris;

rather, it needs to be explored as textured matter that has meaning to all living places. What gives rubble meaning is the awareness of the forces that created this rubble (Gordillo 2014, 5, 8). Alfredo González-Ruibal (2008, 248) sees the study of contemporary destruction as the archaeology of us, or an archaeology of supermodernity, which documents trauma, emotion, and intimate involvement. While most of archaeology focuses on production and consumption, an archaeology of supermodernity is characterized by focusing on destruction as much as on production or consumption. After all, the destruction of the world is rampant, and as some point out, supermodern daily life brings more damage to the world than several world wars (Serres 2000).

Ruins are an invention of modernity and provide a visual reminder of a break with the past (Gordillo 2014, 5, 8; Lowenthal 1985, xviii). For Walter Benjamin, ruins represent the impermanence and destructive tendencies of capitalist culture (Benjamin and Tiedemann 1999). Ruins tear into the spaciotemporal fabric through which new social forms can emerge (Dawdy 2010, 777). Benjamin sees destruction as creative progress. Making room for the future is only made by obliterating the past (Roller 2018a, 29).

The archaeology study presented here is about trauma, destruction, migration, racism, and industrial disasters, all products of unchecked capitalism. Gonzáles-Ruibal (2008, 260) challenges us to think differently about the recent past and think about the destruction that accompanies unchecked capitalism. Otherwise we run the risk of sanctioning what we have done to the world and ourselves: "We need to use archaeology as a tool of radical critique, opposed to ideological mechanisms for sanitizing the past" (González-Ruibal 2008, 261). Therefore, exploring difficult heritage brings to light the conditions of the past, and by connecting these issues to the present, we can make some of these difficult histories a platform from which to discuss the continued prevalence of these inequities. By illuminating and confronting difficult histories we can examine the roots of contemporary social, economic, and political injustices and provide a cause to act on these inequities today (Shackel 2013, 317).

Overview

This book begins with examples from the anthracite coal industry in northeastern Pennsylvania. In the late nineteenth century, American poet and novelist Stephen Crane provided a critique of the working conditions in the anthracite mines. He visited coal mines in the Scranton, Pennsylvania, area in 1894, and his accounts of work there provide an intriguing description of the exploitive conditions that many of the new foreign-born mine workers faced. Those who were not considered equal and not seen as white were easily exploited. In this case it was the Eastern and Southern European immigrant workers. Crane wrote, "Man is in the implacable grasp of nature. It has only to tighten slightly, and he is crushed like a bug." He continued, "If a man escapes the gas, the floods, the 'squeezes' of falling rock, the cars shooting through the little tunnels, the precarious elevators, the hundred perils, there usually comes an attack of 'miner's asthma' that slowly racks and shakes him into the grave" (Crane, quoted in Dublin and Licht 2005, 24). While only visiting the region, Crane's writings show that he was aware of the high fatality rate and the many tragedies that the mine workers faced every day.

Many of the disasters, tragedies, and racism found over a century ago in US industries have been exported to other countries as industries have become increasingly mobile, moving offshore in order to pursue a workforce living in poverty conditions and willing to work (sometimes unwillingly, in a system of slave-like labor) in a system of unchecked capitalism. The research on the anthracite coal mining region of northeastern Pennsylvania provides some valuable information related to health, nutrition, and the everyday existence of the laborers in this industry. While the immigrants faced exploitation and unchecked capitalism, the situation motivated them to organize and protest for better pay and better working conditions. The result of this protest was a labor massacre that left nineteen men dead at the site of the confrontation with the local sheriff and his posse. Press coverage of the 1897 Lattimer massacre and subsequent trial brought the working and living conditions of the anthracite communities to a wider national audience (see Hambidge 1898; Rood 1898). However, the workers and their families received little sympathy or aid, as they were seen as immigrant invaders who were not white and not American. The sheriff and his posse were placed on trial for the killing of the miners and found innocent, marking one of the great miscarriages of the American justice system. Those miners who were associated with the incident were told that they and their family members would never work in the industry again (Novak 1978; Shackel 2018a). A type of historical amnesia fell over the event. The massacre quickly faded from the national public memory, and has disappeared from our history books. The Lattimer massacre of 1897 became known as the Lattimer riots by many after World War I as a result of the backlash against the International Workers of the World (IWW) and the Red Scare. However, in the midst of the ruined anthracite landscape, with abandoned coal breakers and deserted towns, the memory of the event stayed alive under the mainstream currents of public history (Shackel 2018a).

Our work in northeastern Pennsylvania is about understanding the heritage of the place and how people complied with or resisted industrial capitalism. The Roman Catholic Church has a strong connection to labor in the region. Many of the clergy have deep family roots in the mining communities and have experienced poverty, hunger, racism, and environmental degradation as a result of mining. At Lattimer commemorative events, which began in 1972, clergy often connect the era of the massacre to current social justice issues. For instance, at one commemorative anniversary event held at the site of the massacre, the Most Reverend Francis Di Lorenzo, auxiliary bishop of Scranton, compared the social and economic situation of the miners to the present social and economic conditions of the region. He stated, "What is apparently clear to all of us is that these men were actors in a drama which is an eternal drama—an economic drama which we are going through again. Economics was a precipitating part of this violence." He added that, "Many of our people are on the lower end of the wage structure. There is hidden poverty in our area and the distribution of wealth is still a problem" (quoted in McGlynn 1992).

Heritage workers have the power to confront inequalities today. Events of the past can be used to illuminate connections to current social, political, and economic issues. Many of the social injustices that existed in the United States over a hundred years ago still exist or have been exported to other parts of the world. Most large-scale corporations work to make labor inequity invisible, keeping workers and their concerns at the periphery of any discussion related to issues of social justice in the workplace. By bringing to light the conditions of the past and connecting these issues to the present, we can make some of these difficult histories a platform from which to discuss the continued prevalence of these inequities. If we can change the memory of an event, and discuss some of the difficult histories associated with the event, it is possible to change what is important in the public memory, as well as what is significant in contemporary conversations (Little and Shackel 2014).

This book focuses on the remains of the industrial landscape, the rubble and ruins, the casualties associated with industrial ruins. It is about understanding the destructive forces of unchecked capitalism and the forces of race and racism that are so intrinsic in much of our industrial past and present. The first part of this book focuses on the heritage and social justice issues of northeastern Pennsylvania. In the second part of the book, the noticeable link to some of the larger issues of labor exploitation in other regions of the world is discussed. The history of the anthracite coal mining industry in northeastern Pennsylvania is connected to the continuation of labor tragedies in developing countries, in particular, the textile industry in Bangladesh, and the mining industry in South Africa and Turkey.

Chapter 1 focuses on the reliance on immigrant labor in the anthracite coal industry in northeastern Pennsylvania in the late 1800s and early 1900s. Subjected to unequal treatment, relegated to subpar living conditions, and obligated to perform the most dangerous work, immigrants from Southern and Eastern Europe were consistently marginalized and exploited, and were the targets of prejudice and nativist sentiments. The process of racialization and the categorization of people allowed them to be designated as inferior. Racial science that developed as these immigrants arrived from Southern and Eastern Europe supported racist propaganda and nativism that led to the mistreatment of immigrants. Racial categories became part of popular culture and the scientific realm through a variety of studies that started to be published in the middle of the nineteenth century and continued to be institutionalized and reinforced with government documents, like the *Reports of the Immigration Commission* (US Senate 1911b), as well as some eugenics studies in the 1920s. Today, northeastern Pennsylvania's population consists of a well-established, traditional community of descendants of Eastern and Southern Europeans. Their ancestors were part of the last major migration to the United States before federal policies severely limited immigration in the early 1920s through a series of racist laws that were aimed at curtailing the migration from these regions. Northeastern Pennsylvania developed for several generations without any major influxes of outsiders until about 2000, when immigrants began coming to small inland cities like Hazleton, Pennsylvania (Longazel 2016).

Chapter 2 uses a combination of archival records, first-person accounts, secondary sources, and archaeology to provide an overview of the miners' living conditions, vernacular architecture, and arrangement of house and yard space in Lattimer's patch town. Excavations from several households from a coal patch town that was home to Eastern Europeans and Italians provide a micro-view of how scientific racism played out on the household level. Documentation of a congressional hearing features one of the major coal operators discussing his workers in what is now considered a patronizing tone. He bragged that several families can live in a small dwelling that comprises two rooms and a loft containing as many as twelve people. The archaeological excavations investigated the area where Italian immigrants were concentrated, known as the Italian village, and revealed that the residents were relegated to the poorest land, in low-lying areas and on hillside slopes, areas that would have easily flooded due to runoff. An 1898 *Century* magazine article described the shanty village. The original settlement building consisted of salvaged wood, and the community lacked any formal sanitation program. The archaeological record provides important information about the miners' local and traditional practices, including food preservation, gardening, and the creation of terraces, as well as an effort to manage sewage and sanitation. By performing oral histories and archaeology in Lattimer, we are helping to awaken the working-class history of the community (Shackel 2013, 2018a; Roller 2018a).

Chapter 3 describes how coal mining irrevocably transformed the landscape in northeastern Pennsylvania, affecting it in mostly negative ways by contaminating the air, rivers, streams, and drinking water, and destroying vegetation. Pollution from coal mining led to environmental and health problems for local residents in the region. The combination of a toxic landscape and a lack of jobs has led to widespread depopulation in the region, lack of access to nutritious foods, and chronic poverty. Families faced these conditions for several generations, until they could escape from working underground and find steadier employment. Poor living conditions and malnutrition affected the community in the past, and it continues to impact the region today, as the general health and well-being of the northeastern Pennsylvania region still suffers, despite no longer relying on the coal industry for sustenance. Several surveys regarding the region's general health and well-being indicate that this area is the unhappiest place in the United States, a product of the region's declining employment and economic outlook, as well as its poor general health, among other factors. Studies conducted by Gallup and the Centers for Disease Control and Prevention document the poor health and well-being of today's residents of northeastern Pennsylvania. These poor health outcomes could be the result of intergenerational stress that dates to the arrival of immigrants from Southern and Eastern Europe a century ago. Using archaeological assemblages, oral histories, cookbooks, and epigenetic studies, it appears that trauma and structural violence influence the contemporary health and well-being in the region.

Chapter 4 demonstrates how the labor history of northeastern Pennsylvania is not only one that connects history and current events, but also the local and global. Both the mill owners of the past and international corporations of the present seized the opportunity to take advantage of their workforce, paying them low wages and situating them in unsafe working conditions. This exploitation spans the globe as well. Textile mills moved to northeastern Pennsylvania and other places with unorganized labor so that they could operate at a lower cost. Because the families were always close to starvation, the textile operators found labor that was willing to work at significantly lower wages when compared to the organized workforce elsewhere. As the mining industry declined and family incomes shrank, women were willing to work at low-wage industrial jobs in order to help sustain their families. However, as the new workforces unionized and the International Ladies' Garment Workers' Union became powerful, the industry migrated, initially to the American South, then to places like the Commonwealth of the Northern Mariana Islands, where labels could still bear the name "Made in the USA." Until recently, US immigration laws and federal minimum wage laws did not apply to this US territory. Workers were paid subminimum wages until this matter was addressed by the US Congress. By 2009, changes to the immigration and labor laws meant higher wages. As a result, the garment industry moved off the island to other developing countries in South and Southeast Asia. There, workers' health and safety regulations are often ignored, and workers' lives are often in danger. The exploitation of labor in the context of unchecked capitalism has continued throughout history, drawing a parallel between the substandard living conditions, low pay, prohibitive contracts, labor abuses, and dangerous work environments experienced by miners in the past and industrial workers in developing countries today.

Chapter 5 discusses how the labor uprisings in nineteenth- and early twentieth-century US history were not isolated incidents; the exploitation of workers and violent repression of strikes still occur today. On the global scale, workers continue to face poor working conditions and substandard wages. There are two case studies from the twenty-first century to support this argument. First, the Lonmin Marikana platinum mine in South Africa, where striking miners were killed by the South African Police Service in three violent encounters over the course of one month in 2012. Second, in 2014, an explosion in a coal mine in Soma, Turkey, killed 301 mine workers. The push for profit and cost-cutting measures left the mine an unsafe place, which led to the disaster. The leadership of the country referred to the history of mine disasters and explained that the incident was inevitable, which enraged the country. Widespread protests and strikes brought attention to the unsafe working conditions that led to the event, but survivors and their families never received justice. There is a parallel between these modern-day events and the labor practices of nineteenth-century northeastern Pennsylvania, where a desire for greater profits led to a disregard for human life and welfare, resulting in the kinds of tragedies that occurred in each of these case studies.

Framed in the context of its role as a heritage site, the conclusion explains that northeastern Pennsylvania can make significant contributions to the discourse around labor history. As tourism becomes increasingly popular in the region, residents must grapple with the ways in which they will go about commemorating their troubled history. While a group of committed citizens have worked to ensure that the events of the Lattimer massacre do not fade from memory, there remains resistance to these efforts. It is challenging to preserve and promote difficult histories. Rather than covering up or ignoring the decay and ugliness of an industrial landscape, we should confront and acknowledge it as a way to discuss the ugliness of history. These discussions can demonstrate the relevancy of the past—no matter how unpleasant it may be—by drawing parallels between the past and present, such as the coal mines of the nineteenth century and the sweatshops of the twenty-first century.

González-Ruibal (2008, 248) explains that there are three scenarios in which archaeology must produce alternative narratives: (1) genocides and political killing, (2) wars that leave no documentary record or of which the memories are highly contentious, and (3) the subconscious—or unconscious—in culture. In the case of this book, these categories are addressed by focusing on the war on labor and the unnecessary deaths related to those in protest, as well as the casualties related to disasters as a product of unchecked capitalism. In most of the cases outlined in this book, the subconscious and unconscious is related to the racial ideology that has left the working class, past and present, in a position of unequal power.

While the prominence of labor history has faded in the contemporary United States, it is important to rely on this history to place current labor events within the context of a long continuum of efforts for the search for social justice. Connecting the past to the present allows us to address basic human rights, issues related to race and racism, immigration, work, and human dignity and the access to basic human needs. The history of inequality continues to play out on the landscape, in the United States as well as on the global level.

CHAPTER 1
....

The History of Race in the Anthracite Coal Region

Introduction

While anthracite coal was first mined in the Wilkes-Barre region in northeastern Pennsylvania in the late eighteenth century, it was not until the 1820s and 1830s when coal extraction accelerated, making its way to northeastern industries and consumers. The anthracite coal region encompasses about 484 square miles, containing most of the world's supply of anthracite. The coal is located in several narrow bands divided into three fields—southern, middle (sometimes subdivided into eastern middle and western middle), and northern—and they run in a northeasterly direction. Most of the coal is found in seams, or "veins," that can be a few inches to as much as forty to sixty feet thick (Jones 1914, 4–5; Wallace 1987, 5) (Figure 1.1).

In the early nineteenth century East Coast industries began to replace water power with coal, which was seen as a more reliable source of energy. This demand encouraged the coal mining industry's growth and helped to ignite the Industrial Revolution. Northeastern Pennsylvania became an increasingly important region because of its expanding potential to fuel industries. For example, the growing iron industry east of the Alleghenies was fed by the increased output of coal, and as a result, iron became cheaper and more accessible to East Coast industries (Keil and Keil 2015, 7; MacGaffey 2013, 4). From 1870 to about 1920, with the expansion of coal extraction and the influx of new immigrants from Eastern and Southern Europe, the anthracite region became the third-largest population center in Pennsylvania, after Philadelphia and Pittsburgh. The region had twelve mining towns with populations between five and ten thousand residents, and there were sixteen towns that exceeded ten

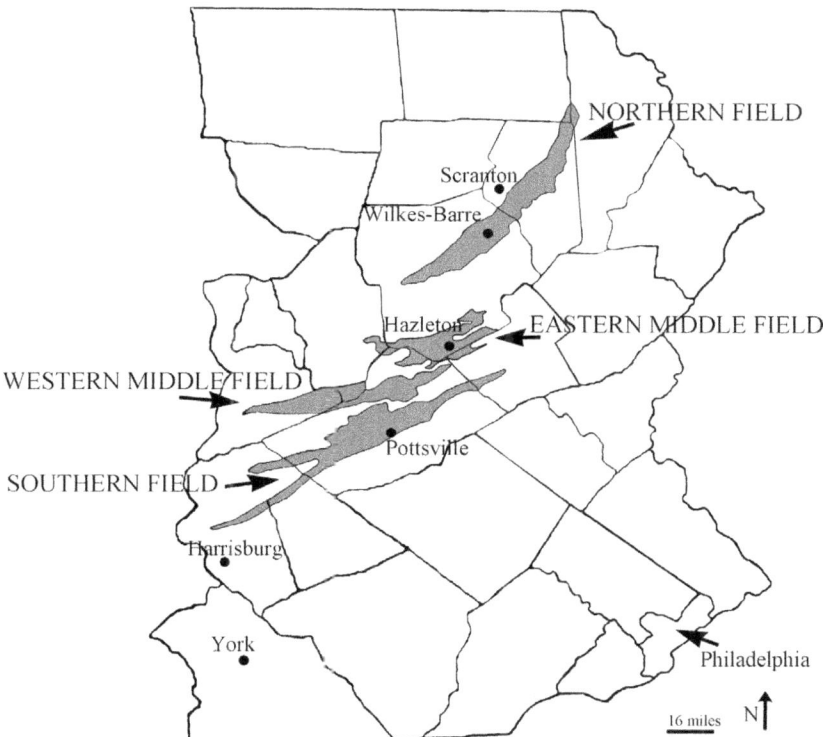

Figure 1.1. Location of the anthracite fields in northeastern Pennsylvania. Drawn by Carol McDavid. Reproduced from Paul A. Shackel, "Immigration Heritage in the Anthracite Coal Region of Northeastern Pennsylvania," *Journal of Community Archaeology & Heritage* 5, no. 2: 101–113, DOI: 10.1080/20518196.2017.1385947, with permission by Taylor & Francis, https://www.tandfonline.com.

thousand people. The largest cities in 1920 included Hazleton (32,000), Wilkes-Barre (73,000), and Scranton (137,000) (Powell 1980, 18). Because of the high profit realized by the coal operators (at the expense of hundreds of thousands of workers), the mined anthracite coal became known as black diamonds.

At the dawn of the anthracite coal extraction, German, English, Scott, and Welsh immigrants comprised the main workforce of the anthracite coal industry. By the middle of the nineteenth century, Irish immigrants escaping the Great Famine joined the workforce and occupied the lower end of the labor hierarchy. In the 1880s and 1890s, Slavic and Italian immigrants began their large-scale migration to the region. The new immigrants from Eastern and Southern Europe increased in numbers from about two thousand in 1880 to over eighty-nine thousand in 1900. In the same time period, the population of those whose families originated in Northern and Eastern Europe remained about the same, at around one hundred thousand. The growing population of Southern and Eastern Europeans created greater competition for jobs, and a new nativistic sentiment developed among the United States' Anglo-Saxon residents (Blatz 2002, 27; Palladino 2006; Turner 1977, 10). The racialization of the new immigrants allowed coal operators to create racial hierarchies in work and allowed for the easy exploitation of "the other" in a system of unchecked capitalism.

The Larger Context of Race

Race and ethnic identity are charged with meaning related to differences and power, although the two identities develop in different ways. Charles Orser (2007, 8) explains that ethnicity is created from the inside, while race is imposed from the outside based on perceived biophysical differences as well as cultural practices, religious beliefs, traditions, and a combination of physical and cultural attributes. Therefore, racialization is the process of assigning people to groups based on physical or cultural characteristics, which helps create the perception of inferior or socially unequal groups. Racialization creates racially meaningful groups that previously did not exist. Those classified as "other" are seen as inferior to the group creating these classifications (Omi and Winant 1983, 51; Orser 2007, 9). The creation of racial categories has led to the unequal ranking of groups of people and the unequal distribution of wealth, as well as the long-term development of health disparities in the region (Shackel 2018b).

Much of the racism and racialization found in the anthracite region has its roots in the scientific racism that developed a few centuries before. Physicians and philosophers in Western Europe began discussing these issues at about the same time that Europeans were discovering new lands and encountering different peoples with different customs and different biophysical traits. They were creating racial hierarchies and evolutionary schemes that justified conquest and subordination. For instance, Francois Bernier (1620–1688), a French physician, published the first racial hierarchical classification in 1684. He divided humankind into five groups based on skin color and other physical characteristics. These groups included Europeans, Africans, Asians, Lapps, and American Indians. Even though Bernier used the term "races," he was a monogenist. He did not regard the different races as unique species (Patterson and Spencer 1994, 22).

In 1735, Swedish naturalist Carolus Linnaeus published the first edition of his *Systema Naturae*. In this volume he placed human beings and apes in the same taxonomic group (Anthropomorpha) because of shared physical characteristics. In subsequent volumes he classified people based on their physical characteristics as well as demeanor. Linnaeus explained that morally and physically the European was considered to be intermediate between the American Indian and the Asian, with the African at the bottom of the series (Patterson and Spencer 1994, 22).

In 1775 and 1795, the German biologist Johann Friedrich Blumenbach, a monogenist, claimed that there were five varieties of human beings, all of which belonged to the same species. These included Caucasian, Ethiopian, Mongolian, American Indian, and Malay. According to Blumenbach, the original stock was Caucasian. The Malays and Ethiopians diverged from the original type in one direction, and the American Indians and Mongolians in another. In 1830, Charles Caldwell, a physician trained at the University of Pennsylvania, argued that God had created four distinct species, which included Caucasians, Mongolians, Indians, and Africans. His works were influential and he became a major figure in the polygenist movement, which had enormous consequences on the development of race theories for many subsequent generations. He further claimed that the Caucasians were the most civilized (Horsman 1981, 118–19). Caldwell and others advocated for the idea that human variation could be explained by separate and distinct creations, thereby challenging the established paradigm of monogenism (Dewbury 2007, 121).

As the discipline of anthropology was forming in the middle of the nineteenth century, its first practitioners tended to be professionals in other fields (e.g., medicine, zoology, biology), and they used their primary discipline to develop their theoretical foundations for anthropology. The early "American school" developed with three theorists who were European-trained physicians: Samuel George Morton, Louis Agassiz, and Josiah Nott. They were strong proponents of polygenism (Dewbury 2007, 127).

Samuel George Morton, trained at the University of Pennsylvania medical school, accepted the authenticity of Blumenbach's racial categories. In his *Crania Americana* (1839), he showed that there was a gradation in the average brain size of the five races, and the differences between Caucasian and Negro cranial capacities had existed since the beginning of humankind on earth (believed at the time to be about four thousand years prior). He wrote that four thousand years was too short to allow for the brain size difference. In 1850, Louis Agassiz (1850, 142–44), in his introduction to Josiah Nott and George Gliddon's *Types of Mankind* (Stanton 1960, 161–73), argued that the white race had at least four subdivisions and that the white race was the most civilized. Agassiz also wrote about the perceived dangers if the races mixed (Patterson and Spencer 1994, 22).

While this science of polygenism was developing in the mid- to late nineteenth century, the new migrants from Eastern and Southern Europe were migrating to the United States in large numbers, and nativists feared they were bringing to the United States different religions, languages, and traditions that did not conform to traditional American expectations. African Americans and Native Americans were seen as too savage to attain citizenship. The Chinese, who came to the American West in the 1860s and 1870s to build railroads, faced similar forms of disenfranchisement, as did the Japanese, Mexican, and Filipino migrants who came to the United States to labor in the agricultural sector (Baker and Patterson 1994, 2). The large influx of unknown and foreign cultures created a fertile ground for the rise of scientific racism and the racialization of the "other" (Allen 1983, 1986; Chase 1980; Pick 1989).

When the Irish Catholics fled the potato famine in the 1840s, they were greeted in the industrial northeast with nativist sentiments and anti-immigration campaigns started by political organizations like the Know Nothings (Baker and Patterson 1994, 2). These immigrants were considered lowbrow, savage, lazy, and wild. The whiteness of the Irish was often questioned, and sometimes black/Irish connections were made explicitly (Roediger 2007, 133). The racism that the Irish were exposed to originated in the British Isles, where the Irish were subjugated by the English and were identified as "Irish savages" in opposition to the English (Orser 2001; Sacks 1989). The categories of race being constructed created social hierarchies and barriers that justified and legitimized existing or emerging relations and practices in the United States.

Anthropology, as a developing discipline, was influenced by this nativist attitude to racialize groups and supported the emerging scientific racism. The discipline created social hierarchies and barriers based on biophysical traits that legitimized social relations. The works of E. B. Tylor (1871, 1881) and Lewis Henry Morgan (1877) advocated the theory of social Darwinism, which aided in creating and reinforcing human racial typologies. Social Darwinism, influenced by Herbert Spencer's theory of evolution, was used by philosophers and the emerging social sciences to support the idea that some groups of people were morally, mentally, and physically superior to others. Tylor's and Morgan's work added a veneer of scientific rationality to bigoted, socially constructed conceptions of race (Thomas 2000, 38–42).

In the 1890s Daniel G. Brinton, a Philadelphia-trained physician who became a professor of ethnology and archaeology at the Academy of Natural Sciences and the University of Pennsylvania, described five races based on a combination of physical and cultural traits. They were white Eurafricans, black Austroafricans, brownish Asians, coppery Americans, and dark insular peoples. Brinton (1890a, 56, 350; 1890b, 47–50, 96–107) used classifications of races that were already being commonly used in political discourse and in newspapers for several decades. He explained that biophysical characteristics differentiated these ethnic groups. These different groups were different races, and a natural hierarchy existed. He argued that there was a clear hierarchical order and that the white race was superior. Britton noted that those closer to civilization were more able to be educated than those living at farther distances, whom he categorized as savages and barbarians. He also created categories of white-skinned buffer races that separated Anglo-Saxon groups from the other darker-skinned subspecies (Patterson and Spencer 1994, 23).

The founders of criminal anthropology in the late nineteenth century, Cesare Lombroso and three of his followers, Giuseppe Sergi, Enrico Ferri, and Alfredo Niceforo, wrote about the inferiority of Southern Italians especially when compared to Northern Italians. Niceforo's best-known work, *Contemporary Barbarian Italy* (1898), extended his thesis of Southern Italian inferiority to Sardinia. Expanding upon Lombroso's work, he noted that there was one Italy, although it could not be unified without changing the course of evolution in the south of the country. He called for two countries that would be divided by race. The south of Italy, Niceforo argued, was not mature enough to govern itself. He explained in *Italians of the North and Italians of the South* (1901) that the Southern Italians were tied to the civilization of the past centuries (D'Agostino 2002, 327). The Southern Italian was portrayed as excitable, impulsive, highly imaginative, and impracticable, an individualist having little adaptability to highly organized society. The Northern Italian, on the other hand, was pictured as cool, deliberate, patient, practical, and capable of great progress in the political and social organization of modern civilization (D'Agostino 2002, 332).

The Immigration Restriction League (IRL) was one of the prime organizations that shaped public opinion about immigration and allowed capitalists to justify treating human resources as expendable, much like the coal operators in northeastern Pennsylvania, as well as elsewhere in the United States. The IRL was founded by three Harvard graduates who were among the Boston Brahmins elite. They were concerned about the growing political power of the Irish. Subsequently, their mission and constituency became much broader, opposing new immigration (Solomon 1956). The organization developed a campaign against the "Slav, Latin, and Asiatic races" (Solomon 1956; Sudarkasa 1968, 158).

Members of the IRL wrote about the progressive and energetic stock of Northern and Western Europeans compared to the historically downtrodden, atavistic, and stagnant stock of the Slav, Latin, and Asiatic races.

Robert Ward, one of the founders of the IRL, wrote that while the new immigrants found employment in many of the growing industries, the real question would be the mental and physical composition of the American population once these new populations began to mix with the Anglo-Saxons (Pavalko 1980, 58). Kenneth L. Roberts, one of the prominent members of the IRL, wrote anti-immigration articles that appeared in the popular press, like the *Saturday Evening Post*. He is known as one of the most effective racist propagandists (Gossett 1963, 402). His book, *Why Europe Leaves Home* (Roberts 1922), was a best seller and is filled with racist propaganda. For instance, he wrote:

> The American nation was founded and developed by the Nordic race, but if a few more million members of the Alpine, Mediterranean and Semite races are poured among us, the results will inevitably be a hybrid race of people as worthless and futile as the good-for-nothing mongrels of Central America and Southeastern Europe. (Roberts 1922, 22)

A large proportion of the new immigrants coming to northeastern Pennsylvania originated from Southern Italy and Eastern Europe, and the work by these social scientists played a major role in establishing how Americans perceived and welcomed the new immigrant into industrial society. The new immigrants were classified and ranked based on country of origin and moved into jobs that they were seen as being capable of doing because of these influential and popular studies.

Race and Jobs in the Anthracite

Job assignments in the anthracite coal industry were mostly based on the racial categories created by the prevalent racialized attitudes conveyed by science and society. The new immigrants could not gain the position of miner until they spent significant time being trained as a helper or a laborer. An anti-immigrant law passed by Pennsylvania legislators in 1889, in an attempt to limit the number of foreign-born miners, required that a worker had to have two years' experience belowground and pass an exam that had twelve questions written only in English in order to qualify as a certified miner. Those coal operators employing uncertified miners could be given stiff fines. This act prohibited many foreign-born laborers from graduating to the position of miner (Greene 1968, 115). This was a form of structural violence that slowed the job advancement of the new immigrants, which would have allowed them to earn a better wage to support their families and stave off starvation (Shackel 2018a).

The average mine workers' compensation decreased significantly over the nineteenth century. One estimate from the Industrial Commission of Transportation (1901, quoted in Greene 1968, 52) calculated that in 1870, miners received $3.00 per day, general laborers $2.00, and breaker boys $0.80. By the end of the nineteenth century wages fell to $2.25, $1.40, and $0.75 a day, respectively. Anthracite coal operators could easily recruit foreigners to the region, as many were fleeing political tyranny and horrendous economic conditions in their home countries. The large-scale migration to the region created a large workforce, usually with more available workers than jobs Surplus labor allowed coal operators to keep wages relatively low with the threat that there were more available hungry men willing to be interchanged into the labor system (Roller 2015).

An 1898 published account in the *Yale Review* documents the anthracite mining employment situation: "It is also because of a definite and conscious purpose among employers to have on hand a full supply of cheapest available labor. 'Wherever I have had a serious strike, one of my best weapons has been to get in foreign workmen,' was the frank admission of one of the mine owners" (J. Brooks 1898, 306). Another coal operator explained that he "must have more men on hand than could be used at any except the best business period," saying, "Our positive management of the more ignorant foreigner cannot be said to have turned out well, because the constant surplus, in times of depression, is open to so many dangers" (J. Brooks 1898, 306).

Throughout much of the 1880s, with the collapse of several unions in the anthracite region like the Knights of Labor, and the beginning of the 1890s, with the establishment of the United Mine Workers of America (UMWA), labor organizations developed to protect the jobs of the established "English-speaking" workers. The Knights of Labor tried organizing the coal workers in the late 1870s and 1880s. The Knights of Labor was dominated by the Irish, while a competing organization, the Amalgamated Association of Mines and Mine Laborers, consisted of mostly American, English, Welsh, and German members. The organizations competed with each other, and neither was welcoming of the new immigrants from Eastern and Southern Europe. Terrance Powderly, an Irish nationalist and a former abolitionist and then Grand Master Workman of the Knights of Labor, wrote in the 1880s about the semibarbarous hordes coming from Hungary to America (Roediger 2005, 14). The Knights of Labor vanished from the anthracite region after the failed strike in 1887/88.

As the number of foreign-born workers increased dramatically, and after a successful attempt by the UMWA to organize foreign-born workers during the Hazleton strike in 1897 (which led to the Lattimer massacre), it became necessary to think differently about the racist goals of unions to protect "English speakers." In 1899, under the leadership of John Mitchell, president of the UMWA (from 1898 to 1908), the organization made a stronger recruitment effort in the anthracite region. By 1900, the UMWA began developing comprehensive strategies, rather than reacting to local disputes. Mitchell developed a cohesive organizational framework, which was disciplined and created a solid front (Yellen 1936, 143–44). "As a result, the UMWA succeeded in uniting fragmented local organizations and limiting the interregional discord and violence that had plagued the region's labor movement in the past" (O'Bannon et al. 1997, 62).

Mitchell did not feel that the union was strong enough to negotiate for a wage increase, nor did they have the resources for a sustained strike. However, in 1900, the bituminous workers in western Pennsylvania received a 20 percent wage increase. The executive board sent Mitchell to seek an agreement with the anthracite coal operators (Miller and Sharpless 1998, 250). The coal operators refused to meet with Mitchell, nor were they willing to recognize the union. On 17 September 1900, the UMWA issued a call to strike. John Mitchell spoke out for a more inclusive UMWA when he exclaimed at the beginning of the 1900 coal strike, "The coal you dig isn't Slavish or Polish, or Irish coal. It's just coal" (quoted in Beik 2002, 67). This phrase became the rallying slogan for the 1900 strike as well as for subsequent actions.

In 1900, around 65 percent of the mine workers were UMWA members. About 125,000 men went on strike, and Mary Harris "Mother" Jones joined the protest. Harris, along with other strike leaders, went from colliery to colliery closing mines. In October 1900, Republican politicians told the coal operators that they needed to meet some of the demands of the union and end the strike immediately, if they wanted to avoid Republican losses in the November elections. They also feared that the strike would spread to the bituminous coal fields in western Pennsylvania. J. P. Morgan, who had significant financial interests in anthracite, also urged the operators to negotiate with the miners. The strike ended on 29 October, when the coal companies conceded to the union's wage demands. The workers also gained the eight-hour workday. John Mitchell's stature grew in the national public view. He was seen as a skillful negotiator who was willing to compromise. The miners proclaimed 29 October a holiday and named it "John Mitchell Day." However, the coal operators did not recognize the union or John Mitchell (Cornell 1957, 39–40; Dulles and Dubofsky 1984, 180–81). The day is still commemorated today in the region among some labor activists and former miners.

Peter Roberts (1901), writing about the strike in his book *The Anthracite Coal Industry*, noted:

> Prophets had predicted that it would be impossible to bring the fourteen or sixteen nationalities into line to effect a strike of any importance. It was done, and it stands to-day as one of the most marvelous achievements of organized labor in the whole world. It was the anthracite coal operators who first brought the Sclavs to the coal fields, to break the power of Anglo-Saxon labor, but these foreigners have proved capable of forming labor organizations which are more compact and united than any which ever existed among the various English-speaking nationalities, who first constituted these communities. (Roberts 1901, 171–72)

After the 1900 victory, the ranks of the UMWA grew dramatically. The operators complied with only some of the demands of the miners. They adhered to a new wage scale, although they did not recognize the miners' committee. Safety improvements were generally ignored by the operators. The coal operators felt that the union might demand subsequent concessions. Some of the companies responded by fencing off the collieries, a type of fortification protecting mines and equipment. They also began stockpiling coal as a guard against any subsequent prolonged strike (Miller and Sharpless 1998, 255).

The Great Coal Strike of 1902

The UMWA met in 1901 and voted to strike if the operators did not recognize the union. Mitchell saw the need for negotiations and compromise, and he stalled any action for a while. The terms of the 1900 contract were about to expire, and when he met with the operators they refused to negotiate with the union. In March 1902, the UMWA met again and voted once more to strike. On 12 May 1902, Mitchell called for a temporary suspension of work in the mines. However, three days later the miners met at Hazleton and voted to continue the strike. More than 147,000 miners walked off the job. It was the beginning of one of the largest strikes in American history. Miners asked for the same terms as two years earlier, including wages that equaled those found in the bituminous region, better safety conditions, and freedoms from the company store (Fink 2015, 55; Foner 1964). Mitchell wrote to Mother Jones about the strike and told her "that the strike will probably be the fiercest strike in the union's history. It will be a fight to the end. The UMWA will either emerge triumphant or be completely annihilated" (quoted in Fink 2015, 57).

The coal miners prepared for a long strike, and the coal operators claimed that the strike was being led by anarchists, the new foreign-born immigrants who had joined the UMWA. John Mitchell held the union together and insisted on nonviolent protests. Since most of the northeast depended upon anthracite coal for heating, as the strike moved into the fall, coal supplies dwindled and the possibility of a coal shortage for the winter started to become a reality.

During the strike, George Baer, the Reading Company's president, wrote a letter to a Wilkes-Barre clergyman who was sympathetic to the strikers. The letter became public and made history. Baer wrote:

> I see that you are a religious man; but you are evidently biased in favor of the right of the workingman to control a business in which he has no other interest than to secure fair wages for the work he does. I beg of you not to be discouraged. The rights and interests of the laboring man will be protected and cared for—not by the labor agitators, but by the Christian men of property to whom God has given control of property rights of country, and upon the successful management of which so much depends. (Quoted in Reynolds 1960, 95)

Baer's letter was released to the newspapers. His divine right argument created a backlash and swayed public opinion away from the coal barons and toward the strikers. Newspapers like the *Chicago Tribune* and the *New York Times* weighed in against the operators. In September 1902, the New York State Democratic Convention met and called for government ownership of the anthracite mines (Miller and Sharpless 1998, 276).

By September, politicians urged President Theodore Roosevelt to work on settling the strike because they feared a backlash in the upcoming election. Mitchell, considered a conservative leader of the union, also became worried when radical organizers gained a foothold in the coal region. Socialist organizers and the anarchist-oriented Industrial Workers of the World (IWW) recruited workers away from the UMWA and to their cause. Mother Jones also reappeared in the anthracite region and led demonstrations and marches. The longer the strike, the stronger the foothold of these alternative labor organizations, which could compromise Mitchell's moderate position (Foner 1964; Miller and Sharpless 1998, 277).

President Roosevelt intervened and tried to encourage arbitration. He summoned the strike leaders and the coal operators to a conference at the White House. Mitchell agreed to abide by the findings of the investigative committee, while George Baer, president of the Reading Company and spokesperson for the operators, refused to arbitrate. Infuriated, Roosevelt told J. P. Morgan that if the operators did not negotiate with the UMWA he would send the army to the coal fields to "dispossess the owners and run the mines as receivers" (Dulles and Dubofsky 1984, 183).

The operators agreed to arbitration by a presidential commission, known as the Anthracite Coal Strike Commission, and the miners went back to work on 23 October 1902, after striking for 163 days. According to Mitchell and members of the UMWA, the labor union was officially recognized by capital and the government. The *United Mine Workers Journal* reported on 30 October 1902 that a convention of seven hundred delegates voted in favor of arbitration by the commission. At the end of the convention, they all sang "My Country 'Tis of Thee." The journal reported, "A score of races mingled in the hall—Saxon and Celt, Teton and Slav, Latin and the native-born—and all joined. One-third of them could not follow the words or melody, but they knew that the hymn was of America, and their hearts sang. The echo of the chorus may well ring through the land, for it is a greeting of free men to a larger freedom that they won for all" (*United Mine Workers Journal* 2007, 5).

The following week, the Anthracite Coal Strike Commission toured the anthracite region to view the conditions of the mine workers. In November and December, the commission heard testimonies from the miners, with Clarence Darrow serving as their attorney (Blatz 1994, 142). The commission announced a 10 percent wage increase and an eight- to nine-hour workday without pay reduction. The commission did not recognize the union (Cornell 1957, 253–254; Wiebe 1961). However, the UMWA became recognized as a force in the region, and many operators recognized the power of the union. The benefits of this new cooperation between labor and capital also led to achieving greater production. At the end of the 1902 strike, Eastern European mining communities and editors of the Polish, Lithuanian, Slovak, and Ukrainian newspapers proclaimed that the "embodiment of everything that is pure, just, right and sublime is John Mitchell" (quoted in Fink 2015, 56).

The 1902 strike was significant for three reasons. First, organized workers won a major victory over one of the most powerful anti-union capitalist groups, the coal barons. Second, during a crucial moment of the strike the workers had the US government siding with the union. And third, it was the first time that a massive strike did not result in the American public condemning the actions of labor as a red menace (Fink 2015, 54).

The 1911 *Reports of the Immigration Commission*

Parts of labor created a united front among its varied constituents, and the outcome of the 1902 anthracite coal strike was an example of uniting all ethnic groups under one union. However, capital continued to work vigorously to divide the working class based on racialized lines. The continued racialization of groups and the momentum and power of the Immigration Restriction League persuaded President Roosevelt in 1907 to create the Immigration Commission. Also known as the Dillingham Commission, its charge was to investigate US immigration issues. In 1911, the US Immigration Commission completed and published a 42-volume report, *The Reports of the Immigration Commission*. The report described the distribution of immigrants throughout the United States and reported on education, crime, employment, insanity, and prostitution, among other topics (Pavalko 1980, 60). The document included testimony and reports from anti-immigration groups. The Patriotic Order Sons of America had 95,000 members in Pennsylvania and smaller numbers in twenty-one other states. They expressed their fear of the new immigrants' impact on American life and urged Congress to "restrict desirable and less assimilative aliens" (quoted in Pavalko 1980, 62).

Economists (R. Smith 1886, 1887; Walker 1891, 33–38) explained how businesses used immigrant labor to depress wages, yet at the same time supported limitations on immigration. Even though the Immigration Commission went to great lengths to describe and classify different races of people, it recommended that any immigration policy be based on economic or business considerations. In Volume 1, the introduction to the study, the document stated that there was an oversupply of unskilled labor and that conditions existed that warranted the restriction of unskilled labor. The Immigration Commission suggested that immigration could be controlled by establishing quotas per year, requiring that the new immigrant have a specific amount of wealth when coming to the country, or having a tax on each person entering the country. The Immigration Commission also recommended that the federal government implement a literacy test to help restrict new immigration (US Senate 1911a, 47–48).

The *Reports of the Immigration Commission* (US Senate 1911a, 274–79) characterized the immigration issue at the turn of the nineteenth century in the following way:

> The Slavic, the Teutonic, and the Italian or Latin are the three great stocks that furnish the most of the population of Europe as well as of our annual flood of immigrants. Of these three, the Slavic and the Italic have been rapidly replacing the Teutonic in American immigration, and the Slavic is perhaps the most significant for the future because of its great population. (See also Caucasian and Aryan and cf. Slovenian.) Physically, and perhaps temperamentally, the Slavs approach the Asiatic, or particularly the Tartar, more closely than do the peoples of Western Europe. In languages they are as truly Aryan as ourselves. . . . If the Slav be still backward in western ideas, appliances, and form of government, it is nevertheless conceivable that the time is not far distant when he will stand in the lead. The race is still young. Its history is shorter than that of any other important people in Europe.

Much of this work relied on the scientific racism scholarship that was popular at the time. Two anthropologists, Daniel Folkmar and Elnora Folkmar, produced *The Dictionary of Races or Peoples* (Volume 5) for *The Reports of the Immigration Commission* (US Senate 1911b). The dictionary deals with the history, language, religion, and physical characteristics of groups and identifies over six hundred races of people (Pavalko 1980, 61). Folkmar and Folkmar followed the racial hierarchy adopted by Daniel Brinton (1890a, 1890b), who used Friederich Blumenbach's eighteenth-century scheme. The schema created five races—the Caucasian, Ethiopian, Mongolian, Malay, and American and known in the vernacular as white, black, yellow, brown, and red (D'Agostino 2002, 327).

The Dictionary of Races or Peoples claimed Northern Europeans were the purest race. However, Folkmar and Folkmar deviated from Brinton's categories and further divided Italians into "Celtic" and "Iberic" groups, following Sergi (and hence Niceforo), separating the group into Northern and Southern Italians (D'Agostino 2002, 331). The Southern Italian was described as a long-headed, dark, Mediterranean race of short stature. They were closely related to the Iberians of Spain and the Berbers of Northern Africa. The document noted that the Southern Italian may have some infusion of blood from Africa (US Senate 1911b, 3, 8). They were said to be "vivid in imagination, affable, and benevolent, but excitable, superstitious, and revengeful" (US Senate 1911b, 127). The Northern Italian was described as "cool, deliberate, patient, practical, and . . . capable of great progress in the political and social organization of modern civilization" (US Senate 1911b, 32). The Slav was identified as incorporating "carelessness as to the business virtues of punctuality and often honest, periods of besotted drunkenness among the peasantry, unexpected cruelty and ferocity in a generally placid and kindhearted individual" (US Senate 1911b, 129).

The Reports of the Immigration Commission (US Senate 1911a) created clear boundaries between the new and old immigrants. Throughout the document, there were references to the lack of mental and physical capacity in the new immigrants (Handlin 1950, 82). The document stated that the English and Irish came to the United States "imbued with sympathy for our ideals and our democratic institutions." The "Norse" make "ideal farmers and are often said to Americanize more rapidly than do the other peoples who have a new language to learn." Indeed, "the German is too well known in America to necessitate further discussion." By contrast, the Serbo-Croatians have "savage manners." Although the "Poles verge toward the 'northern' races of Europe," being lighter in color than the Russians, "they are more high-strung, resembling the Hungarians" in that respect (US Senate 1911b, quoted in Roucek 1969, 44).

Reaction to Scientific Racism

Scientific racism during the nineteenth century was mostly unchallenged, allowing for the exploitation of many of the new immigrants. However, by the beginning of the twentieth century, the work of Lombroso as well as the work of other proponents of scientific racism was increasingly being challenged. For instance, in 1900, Frances Kellor wrote "Criminal Sociology: The American vs. The Latin School" in the *Arena*. Kellor explained that Lombroso did not consider "environmental forces," which should include climate, food, light, heat, governmental and economic conditions, occupations; also parental influences, training, education, culture, and opportunities. Kellor argued that Lombroso's exclusive reliance on only anthropometric data led to skewed results (1900, 301–4).

Franz Boas became a major voice in challenging the dominant paradigm that immigrants from Southern Europe were inferior to the white "American stock" (Boas [1906] 1974, 1910, 1940, 1945; see also Baker and Patterson 1994, 2; Benedict 1940). As early as 1894, Boas spoke out against racial classifications and hierarchies. His article, "Human Faculty as Determined by Race," explains that we should not assume that one race is more highly gifted than the other (Liss 1998, 131). He questioned the notion that race was biologically fixed and permanent and that people could be ranked in proximity to apes (Mukhopadhyay and Moses 1997, 518). He continued to challenge the dominant paradigm well into the twentieth century. In 1911, the Universal Races Congress was held in London, attended by W. E. B. Du Bois and Franz Boas, along with 2,100 other participants. It was part of a growing movement to challenge the scientific racism that had taken hold in popular culture and the academy. Boas provided scientific proof regarding the impact of the environment on human forms, stressing the plasticity of physical characteristics (Boas 1911a, 1912). Boas's *The Mind of the Primitive Man* (1911b) was an important publication that made cultural relativism and multiculturalism foundational concepts in anthropological thinking. He stressed the importance of environment over heredity in creating human populations. The work challenged the celebration of Western civilization and stressed the importance of other cultures and experiences as valid cultural expressions (Roseberry 1992, 848; Visweswaran 1998, 70). In *Changes in Bodily Form of Descendants of Immigrants* (1912), Boas demonstrated that morphological features, including such core racial indicators as head form, could change in a single generation because of nutritional, environmental, or cultural factors (Blakey 1987; Mukhopadhyay and Moses 1997, 518). Paul Rabinow (1992, 60) claims that "Boas' arguments against racial hierarchies and racial thinking have thoroughly carried the theoretical day."

Julia Liss (1998, 20) notes that "the implications of these findings—an antideterminist view of difference that, combined with Boas's own assimilationist leanings, suggested a new basis for coexistence—were as ignored at the time as they were revolutionary."

It would take several generations before his observations would have a significant impact on twentieth-century views of race. While critiques of scientific racism were led by Boas, it was not until the next generation of scholars, led by Ruth Benedict (1940) and Ashley Montagu (1942), that the dominant paradigm began to change (Harrison 1998, 617). Anthropologists argued against the old classifications of racial construction and supported a socially and culturally constructed concept of race. Some scholars note that during this era some of the not-quite-white ethnics became white. Italians were usually considered a buffer race and held a position between whites and blacks. They did not receive full recognition of Caucasian status until the World War II era (Luconi 2016, 188). In the 1950 US federal census, the ethnicity, place of birth, and nationality of parents were no longer recorded (Sacks 1989).

Historian Oscar Handlin (1957, 80–81), in his book *Race and Nationality in American Life*, challenged the findings of *The Reports of the Immigration Commission*, noting that the committee took for granted the results of the scientific racism of the era that was prevalent in the academy and in popular culture. In 1952, the United Nations Educational, Scientific, and Cultural Organization rejected the linkage between sociocultural differences and biology (Mukhopadhyay and Moses 1997, 519). Sherwood Washburn's (1963) presidential address to the American Anthropological Association in 1962 rejected the validity of race as a *biological* category and focused instead on the concept of a population (Haraway 1989, 197–206). Furthermore, Montagu argued that race was a socially constructed category that continued to provide an essential underpinning for racism. Sociologists and social historians—including Nathan Glazer and Daniel Moynihan (1963; Moynihan 1965), and Oscar Handlin (1957)—also downplayed the importance of race as a biological category, arguing instead for the importance of culture and ethnicity in the constitution of everyday life. Yet although race is no longer a scientifically credible position in anthropology, racism has hardly disappeared from the American landscape (Rabinow 1992, 60).

Conclusion

American industrialists depended on nonwhite foreigners as industrial workers as well as consumers, and at the same time they despised them as "primitives" in need of civilizing. They were considered a threat to the national order and Anglo-Saxon culture of the United States (Jacobson 2001). Creating a racialized view of the new immigrant allowed for the easy exploitation of the newcomers.

David Roediger (2005, 53) points out that the boundaries between white and nonwhite were not always clear, and some exclusionary rhetoric stopped short of condemning a whole race. "Instead [they] argued that the particular poverty-stricken segments of the population migrating were made unfit for citizenship by history as much as biology." It was not until after the enactment of the 1920s anti-immigration legislation that the United States moved from a variety of races to monolithic whiteness, and eventually all Europeans were categorized as Caucasian. The expanded definition of Caucasian was created in opposition to nonwhites (Jacobson 1998, 93–135).

The success of the UMWA in the anthracite region might have pointed the way to a more inclusive rank and file. However, many labor leaders continued to demand immigration restriction. For instance, in 1902, Samuel Gompers, founder and president of the American Federation of Labor (AFL), backed a literacy test for immigrants. According to Gompers, such tests would keep relations with English-speaking immigrant nations intact and would slow the immigration of the Slavs (Roediger 2005, 81). In the 1920s Congress granted this wish. In 1968, Victor Greene wrote:

> Labor leaders then and perhaps now tend to overlook the fact that the work force is a part of America's pluralistic society. In the past, rather than trying to limit the numbers of component ethnic groups, for their own benefit unions should have accepted this country's heterogeneity. They should have conformed their tactics to the cultural habits of those that they wished to attract. Even today, by refusing to recognize the more self-conscious minorities, mass associations will stagnate, never to expand with the growing rank and file. (Greene 1968, 215)

CHAPTER 2

An Archaeology of Immigration, Race, and Poverty in the Anthracite Coal Region

Background

Since 2009, the Anthracite Heritage Project has been performing archaeology in several coal patch towns in the anthracite region of northeastern Pennsylvania. While primary resources and oral histories make the region's past accessible, the archaeology provides a different perspective about everyday life in the region. While much has been written about the coal industry, very little has been revealed about the life in the region on a micro-scale. In particular, the archaeology exposes how race and racialization of populations impacted the everyday lives of workers and their families. How families coped in this racialized society becomes an important question and allows us to reflect upon the conditions in which the descendants of these early immigrants survive today.

Race and Slavic Immigration

Much of our work in the Anthracite Heritage Project focuses on communities that are of Italian and Slavic decent. Those of Slavic background received a significant amount of attention and study by the prominent social scientists of the day, and derogatory stories about the new Eastern European immigrants were common. Slavs were stereotyped as having practiced wife selling as well as polyandry. They were also blamed for a higher crime rate and considered more dangerous than the Chinese. (The United States passed anti-Chinese immigration laws in the 1880s.)

The Slav was believed to freely use dynamite on the home of anyone whom they did not like or trust (Turner 1977, 11). In 1885, in a report of the Iowa Bureau of Labor Statistics, a laborer expressed his racial opinions in terms of whiteness. He explained that "the Bohemians . . . will get a job in preference to a white man" (quoted in Pavalko 1980, 61).

In a 1904 account, Peter Roberts, a sociologist and prominent scholar on Slavic migration, reinforced the dominant sentiments of the times about Eastern and Southern European immigrants. He wrote:

> We need men and women who harmonize with national ideals and character, which is of greater importance than the pecuniary gain. The thousands of immigrants added to our population have lowered our standards of living, have bred discontent, and have brought elements that are utterly un-American in ideas and aspirations into our communities. These, by their adherence to their language and customs, remain unassimilated after years of residence in the United States. This works disintegration in our industrial and social life and, unless counteracting forces are set in motion, will result in a lower type of manhood and womanhood in these communities. (Roberts [1904] 1970, 345)

A few years earlier, in 1900, the *New York Herald* described the Slavs as being backward, uncivilized, and clannish. The writer illustrated a Sabbath celebration with some contempt:

> You will find the worst specimens of humanity to be found anywhere in the world. The habitués of these resorts are the off-scourings of Europe—brigands of the Carpathian Mountains, and the murderers of rural Hungary and the Russian Steppes. The men who constitute the choice convivial spirits of these murky, smoke-colored rooms are no farther along in human progress than were their ancestors, the hordes of Attila, when he led them howling up to the gates of Rome. These grimy saloons . . . present little pictures of a life that is not of this age. . . . They carry you back into the Burgundian taverns of the fourteenth century, into the bandits' den of Upper Hungary. (Quoted in Greene 1968, 114)

The *Dictionary of Races* describes the Serbo-Croatians as having savage manners, being illiterate, and being at a low stage of civilization (US Senate 1911b, 47). In a published chapter in the *Second International Congress of Eugenics Held at the American Museum of Natural History, New York, September 22–28, 1921,* Paul R. Radosavljevich (1923) wrote about the "Eugenic Problems of the Slavic Race." He mentioned that "the Slavs have always toiled for others, suffering and dying for the Christian humanity" (Radosavljevich 1923, 158). He later explained, "External trimmings do not very much attract the Slavs. They do not show a desire to advance themselves in the material ways that come to mean so much to the western world. They are able to live without the comfort of Englishmen, without the finaries of the French; they are satisfied with simplicity; they do not care for luxuries and above all things they like a warm soul and a sincere heart" (Radosavljevich 1923, 159).

In referring to the Slav's sentimentality and stoicism, Radosavljevich (1923, 162–63) notes that "the lack of sentimentality, submission to fate and willingness to experience a failure when it is necessary, of course, is the most characteristic form of slavic suffering. . . . No race knows better than the Slavic how to suffer and what suffering means. This suffering makes the Slavs compasionate. . . . It knows how to suffer, and therefore, it knows how to bear suffering with a high degree of stoicism, and then, it knows how to inflict it with insensibility when occasion arises" (Radosavljevich 1923, 162–63).

Many immigrants coming from the Austro-Hungarian Empire were often referred to as "hunkies." Classifications at the turn of the twentieth century divided the Slavs into three groups according to territories. The eastern Slavs were "the Great Russians, the White Russians, and the Little Russians, or Ruthenians." In the western portion of the Slavic territory were "found the Poles, the Bohemians, the Moravians, the Slovaks and the Serbs." On the southern portion of the territory were "found the Serbians or Serbs, Croatians, Bosnians, Montenegrins, Slavonians, Dalmatians, Slovenes, Bulgarians, and Macedonians" (P. Roberts [1904] 1970, 27–28).

In 1870, the Slavs comprised about 1 percent of the immigrants to the United States. By the first decade of the twentieth century they consisted of about 28 percent of the immigrant population (P. Roberts 1912, 38). In 1904, Roberts described the Slavic mining population in the anthracite region: "His intellectual capacity clogged 'by the weight of the centuries' is not equal to that of the German and the British workman. . . . The Russians . . . are a few centuries behind the rest of the civilized world" (P. Roberts [1904] 1970, 25). The author then stated that the Slav showed promise of social progress and assimilation. "The Sclav is a good machine in the hands of competent directors. He is obedient and amenable to discipline, courageous and willing to work, prodigal of his physical strength and capable of great physical endurance. . . . He thinks slowly and is willing to follow the lead of others, but when the Sclav is once set in motion in a given course, he is there to stay" (P. Roberts [1904] 1970, 36). In 1912, Roberts later wrote about the Slav in the anthracite region in terms of whiteness. "The seams changed, there was more brawn needed, more powder per ton of coal must be burned, and 'white men' refused to work under conditions that meant more labor, more expense, and less pay. Then they called in the willing Slav, the submissive Lithuanian, and the work was done" (P. Roberts 1912, 55).

Slavic Living Conditions

Joseph Roucek (1976, 58) notes that while only a minority of the Slavs brought with them ideas of socialism and a radical ideology, they were labeled as an undesirable racial category. This labeling was justification for these lower groups to send their children into the beakers and the coal mines. As a result, in the mining districts of Pennsylvania child labor among the Slavs exceeded all other ethnic groups. Parents often falsified their children's ages on work permits, which placed children in labor situations much earlier than other groups. Their labor was expected to make a significant contribution to the sustenance of the household as well as contribute to its material support. The 1911 *Report on Conditions of Women and Child Wage Earners in the United States* indicates that in Scranton, Pennsylvania, 35 percent of a Polish family's income in 1911 was earned by children (Bodnar 1982, 46).

Since Slavic children were sent to work by their families, their school attendance ranked lowest in the United States. The 1911 national study indicates that Slovaks and Poles had the smallest percentage of children attending school past sixth grade. In cities like Chicago and Cleveland, only 4 percent of Slovak children were in school. Poles ranked the lowest in places like Buffalo and Scranton, and next to last in Cleveland and Milwaukee. Slovak children were noticeably absent from public high school. For instance, in Chicago, about 5 percent of African American children attended high school, while only 1 percent of Poles and Slovaks attended high school (Bodnar 1982, 48).

The US Department of Labor's *Children's Bureau, Publication 106* (1922) report summarized the poor health conditions in the anthracite region. Because of the poverty and the general poor living conditions in these coal patch towns, the infant mortality rate was extremely high, and in some places five times higher than the US average (US Department of Labor 1915, 9). In 1917, the infant mortality rate in the United States was 94 per 100,000 births. In the town of Shenandoah in the anthracite region, it was 184 per 100,000 births, one of the highest in the country. The average annual death rate related to diarrhea and enteritis among children age two and below in Shenandoah was 365.8 per 100,000 children, while the average for Pennsylvania stood at 104.8, compared to 71.4 for the United States. The rate for diphtheria and croup was four times higher and scarlet fever twelve times higher in Shenandoah when compared to the average in the United States (US Department of Labor 1922, 47).

John Bodnar (1982, 59) explains that high child mortality rate was an expected tragedy in these communities. He uses a study of the Johnstown community to describe this phenomenon. It states,

> Mother aged 31 years, 10 pregnancies in 10 years, 8 live born; 2 still born; 4 deaths in first year.
>
> Mother aged 30 years, 9 pregnancies in 11 years; 8 live births, 1 miscarriage reported, 3 deaths in first year due to pneumonia, malarial fever and rheumatism.
>
> Mother aged 35 years, 6 births in 12 years, 4 live births and 2 still births. All live born died in first year . . . says she had always worked too hard, keeping boarders in this country and cutting wood and carrying it and water on her back in the old country.

The US Department of Labor's *Children's Bureau, Publication 9* report (1915, 9) noted that the contributing factors of the high child mortality rate are related to "underpaid fathers, overworked and ignorant mothers, and poor living conditions."

Racism, Housing, and the New Immigrant in the Anthracite Region

The new immigrants usually came to poorly constructed company towns that were adjacent to the mining operations. The typical patch town consisted of a row of houses along a single road built on company land. The coal company owned the houses, company stores, schools, and churches, as well as the streets. They dictated the community's laws and regulations, and hired their own security force, which eventually became known as the Coal and Iron Police. The workers' houses were usually comprised of duplexes, known in the region as double houses. Additional streets were laid out as new immigrants and their families came to town in search of jobs, and in the case of the new immigrant, they were sometimes responsible for constructing their own shelter. The supervisors lived in a separate section of town, often on higher ground in view of the town so that they could keep surveillance of the working community. The company store usually stood in the middle of the community. Miners and their families paid inflated prices for goods at these stores. After deducting rent, merchandise purchased at the company store, and a fee for a company doctor, the miners and their families were often left with little or no money for the rest of the month. Miners viewed this exploitation as a form of servitude (Miller and Sharpless 1998, 142–43; Shackel 2018c).

At the turn of the twentieth century, Peter Roberts ([1904] 1970) wrote about the built environment and the living conditions of these new immigrants in the anthracite region. The anthracite coal operators, he noted, placed workers and their families in small houses, even for the times. About 70 percent of the new immigrants were male, and the wife and children followed after the laborer established himself in the community. It was common for a family—typically a husband and a wife with two children—to rent to up to ten boarders (single males) at one time. Between four and five people occupied a room, often sleeping in shifts while others worked in the mines. The house rent averaged $4–6 per month and may have been as high as $7 per month, depending on the size of the house. Each boarder paid $1 per month for rent, and there was an extra fee if the woman of the house washed the miner's back each evening. Each boarder also paid for food, which averaged about $5 per month (Roberts [1904] 1970, 90, 105).

As a result of a six-month strike in 1887/88, Eckley B. Coxe, one of the largest coal operators in the eastern middle section of the anthracite region, testified before the US House of Representatives and was recorded in the *Testimony to Investigating Committee, U.S. House of Representatives*. The congressional hearings focused on the fuel shortage and the devastating impact the strike had on industry as well domestic heating in the Mid-Atlantic region. Coxe was asked to describe the housing and living conditions in his company town. He explained, with apparently no regret or shame, that for 35 cents, a miner could rent "some sort of shanty" fit for a bachelor. Coxe also explained: "A family, for $4/Month, could share a four room dwelling with three other families, two upstairs and two on the ground floor, plastered and whitewashed, with a communal kitchen. More generous quarters could be had for $5.50/month, the price of sharing three rooms upstairs and two down with just one other family. These units cost the company $850 to build, and with a monthly rental income of $11, paid for themselves, including repairs, in 6–8 years" (quoted in Holt 2001, 10). He noted that the houses had "good cellars" and plaster interior walls (Holt 2001, 10). The crowded conditions apparently did not faze Coxe or the House of Representatives committee, most probably because the new immigrants were not seen as equal, or even as human. In a personal letter to Terrence Powderly, union leader of the Knights of Labor, labor organizer William Wilson (also of the KOL) described a shanty house:

> Just picture to yourself a little shanty 12 x 16 feet in size, a little bed in one corner and an old cracked cook stove in another, a few rickety chairs placed here and there about the room, bare rough boards for a wall and a cupboard that contains but a few dishes and a half loaf of bread; no butter, no meat, no sugar, no tea or coffee, no nothing but a dry crust of bread. Then after having examined the room turn again to the old rusty stove and see huddled around its faintly glowing embers, a pale faced mother and her six pinched, gaunt and famished children, the youngest nursing from a breast that contains no nourishment. (Quoted in Arnold 2014, 124)

Peter Roberts ([1904] 1970) described the general racialized tones of the era and admits that the new immigrants from Eastern Europe faced racial discrimination. He explained that the racial divide created during the era created an unequal distribution of housing, which helped to form a racially divided and segregated town. He also referred to the Slav as not being white:

> The Sclavs did not in all instances voluntarily take the cheaper houses. They are considered socially inferior to the Anglo-Saxons and Germans, and where there is a variety of dwellings, the first choice is given the English-speaking, and what remains goes to the Sclavs. In a mining camp in the Southern coal fields, a dilapidated and ill-built section was assigned to the "foreigners," while the better houses were occupied by Anglo-Saxons. The Sclavs complain bitterly of their houses, and they had just reason to do so. They said, "me pay more for good house," and most of them would gladly move to better houses were they available. It is the same in our towns. The most dilapidated sections are assigned the Sclavs. He is driven there by social and racial discrimination, and it is only when houses are vacant and no "white tenants" can be secured, that the most respectable and most ambitious Sclavs are able to move into better homes and be surrounded by a purer and healthier environment. In towns where opportunity is given them to buy real estate, many of them secure homes of their own, which are healthier and better than the dwellings found in the leprous sections of mining towns. (Roberts [1904] 1970, 88)

Describing the interior of a Slav household, Roberts ([1904] 1970, 93) also wrote about how the material culture is reflective of racial discrimination and the unequal distribution of resources and wealth.

> The cooking stove is generally brought at a junk shop. The cooking utensils are few and tinware often serves as a substitute for crockery. A common kitchen table and chairs to match complete the furnishings on the first floor, if made up of one room. If there are two rooms, then the front room has one or two beds in it; no carpet and no bedroom suite of "eight pieces." When shown one of these rooms, we had to sit on the trunk of one of the boarders, for there were no chairs there. The room or rooms on the second floor have beds in them and a few trunks. If a heating stove is purchased, it is old fashioned bell-shaped kind, bought second hand, which is a good heater, and the practical Sclav heat and not nickel plate and polish. (Roberts [1904] 1970, 93)

Roberts explained that the houses tended to be constructed of hemlock boards. The walls and ceilings were not plastered, and weather strips were nailed over the crevices—a board and batten construction. The better houses had two rooms on the first floor and one on the second. He described the rooms as shells of about sixteen by sixteen feet (Roberts [1904] 1970, 125).

In 1898, the *Century*, a popular quarterly, described the housing in Lattimer No. 2 during an investigation of living conditions in the region. Henry Edward Rood (1898, 809), a journalist who spent considerable time writing about the life of miners in the region, noted that the English-speaking miners lived in small unpainted frame double houses, and a fence surrounded each property. The houses were built in the same design with the same number of doors and windows, all had the same slanted roof, and the chimneys were all in the same location. Livestock were common in many of the yards, with some households having chickens, and others ducks (Rood 1898, 814).

Ethnography and Archaeology in Lattimer No. 2

Most coal patch towns in the anthracite region had similar housing stock that ranged from smaller double houses to larger single-family homes. (Coal patch towns that surrounded a colliery often had the same name and were numbered. In the case of Lattimer, the patch towns associated with this colliery were numbered 1 and 2. Lattimer No. 1 is now known as Lattimer Mines and Lattimer No. 2 is now known as Pardeesville.) Peter Roberts ([1904] 1970, 129) described the housing situation in Lattimer No. 2. On the east side of the mines, he explained, were the larger houses of four rooms that also had a garret and cellar. These were rented at $5 per month. On the west side of the colliery were two-room shacks that varied from ten by twelve feet to ten by seven feet and rented for between $2 and $3 per month. About a quarter mile separated the two sections (Figure 2.1).

In Pardeesville, our project focused on the west side of the town, which was characterized as having the smaller two-room shacks on a road that was once known as Main Street and later Church Street. (When Pardeesville lost its post office in the 1990s, mail delivery was then provided by the greater Hazleton post office. Since Hazleton already had a Church Street, one of the members of the county council decided to rename the street after a recently deceased pet dog named Scamper.)

Throughout much of its existence, Lattimer No. 2 had a population of about five hundred residents. It developed in two phases, initially settled by Eastern Europeans and soon after by Italians. The initial Slav migration to the town moved to the company-built double houses on the east side. They were constructed in neat and orderly rows and symmetrical in form. The Italian village on the west side became the center of Lattimer

Figure 2.1. Circa 1900 map of Lattimer No. 2 (now named Pardeesville). The eastern portion of the planned town was originally settled by Eastern Europeans. The organic settlement in the northwestern portion of the town was settled by Italian immigrants and known as the Italian village. Copy of 1900 map, Paul A. Shackel.

No. 2's Italian immigrant population. It developed much more organically. The streets meander according to the contours of irregular property boundaries, and the topography and the houses do not conform to any one building plan. Italian immigrants began settling in this portion of Lattimer No. 2 as early as the 1870s. Apparently, the Lattimer Coal Company charged a land rent and the new immigrants constructed their own houses, which were originally ramshackle in nature. With the Slavs living on the east side of town in company-built houses, the Italians initially lived in self-built shacks on the west side of town. An informant told us that the ethnic groups did not mingle (Roller 2018a). One resident of Italian ancestry explained that the "Slavs tended to stay by themselves. They seemed to be much quieter than the Italians."

Beginning in 1879, the Italian newcomers to Lattimer No. 2 celebrated the feast of their patron saint, St. Nazarius. Mass was held in a tent for about five years, and then in 1884 a small chapel was erected and established as a mission church of St. Gabriel, which supplied a priest for twenty years. In 1904, the congregation was large enough to support its own priest. That same year the church was enlarged, and again enlarged five years later, in 1909. In 1947, a new church was constructed "on top," outside of the original Italian enclave, to accommodate the larger congregation. "On top" refers to the ridge, or the high point of the community, which tends to be much drier and does not have the runoff water issues experienced by those living in the Italian village. In 2009, the churches in the Hazleton area were consolidated and the St. Nazarius parish was merged with Our Lady of Grace Church, along with several other coal patch town churches, including St. Mary's Church of Lattimer Mines (Our Lady of Grace Church 2009).

The migration of Italians to northeastern Pennsylvania, and to Lattimer No. 2 in particular, occurred during the larger national debate regarding immigration from Southern and Eastern Europe. For instance, in 1887, the Evangelical Alliance met to discuss issues related to the new Italian immigration. H. H. Boyesen commented on newcomers from Naples and Sicily: "I have, during the past year, again and again seen the Battery Park black with these creatures (in fact, preternaturally black), and the odors which surround them turned the milk of human kindness within me, and made me marvel at the heedless hospitality of the American nation, which was willing to mingle this coarse and brutal strain in their own fresh and vigorous blood" (quoted in D'Agostino 2002, 337). In the American South, communities of Southern Italians were disenfranchised, similar to African Americans. Southern Italians were excluded from white schools, social organizations, and labor unions (Guglielmo 1999, 174).

The Italian ambassador in Washington DC acknowledged that his own fellow countrymen held "a racial middle ground between whites and blacks" in the United States (Luconi 2016). The *Reports of the Immigration Commission* argued that Northern Italians were closely related to the Alpine race and were therefore similar to Anglo-Saxons (US Senate 1911b, 82; Luconi 2016). The Committee on Immigration and Naturalization of the US House of Representatives noted that Southern Italians were not "full-blooded Caucasian"; the *Reports of the Immigration Commission* explained that they were not Caucasian because they likely had an infusion of African blood (US Senate 1911b; US House of Representatives 1912). US Senator John L. Burnett of Alabama stated to the Immigration Commission that "the southern Italian is not a 'white man,' nor is the Syrian" (quoted in Pavalko 1980, 61).

Much of this sentiment supported the eugenics movement (Barkan 1992). Edward Ross, a progressive sociologist who flirted with eugenics in the 1920s, wrote about the supposed backwardness and inferiority of Southern and Eastern Europeans. Ross described these new immigrants as "low-browed, big faced persons of obviously low mentality . . . clearly belong in skins, in wattled huts at the close of the Great Ice Age. These ox like men are descendants of those who always stayed back" (quoted in Guglielmo 1999, 193). He wrote in the *Century* magazine (Ross 1914, 440), "Steerage passengers from a Naples boat show a distressing frequency of low foreheads, open mouths, weak chins, poor features, skew faces, small or knobby crania, and backless heads." He explained that "such people lack the power to take rational care of themselves." Others wrote about "race suicide" and demanded restrictions on immigration as well as the implementation of a literacy test.

In the midst of this debate on immigration, Italians and Slavs came to Lattimer No. 2 eager to work in the mines. Church Street was the center of the Italian village, with the St. Nazarius church as the focal point. An alley ran adjacent to the church and intersected Church Street. A set of shanty-like houses stood adjacent to and across the street from the church. The house sizes and shapes varied for each lot. In 1898, Jay Hambidge described the condition of the Italian village:

> The company houses in No. 2 are few, and we are soon at the opening of a lane much narrower and more crooked than the one we have just traversed. It leads into the patch, and up this lane we drive. Then up another lane, more tangled than the last; and this is the principal street of a settlement of the queerest structures, some of them not much larger than dog-kennels. . . . This is a place to be described by metes and bounds and degrees of instruments, and to do it would tax the ingenuity of the best of surveyors. Can you read character from handiwork? If so, this would be a place to practice your art. Each little house, with the boxes, cubby-holes, and fences about it, has been built by the man who lives in it. (Hambidge 1898, 824)

Some company operators, like Calvin Pardee, owner of Lattimer No. 1 and Lattimer No. 2, leased land so that miners could build their own dwellings. Workers could also lease land to plant a vegetable garden. Pardee charged 50 cents a month rent for land. Men built their own shanty and enclosed it with a fence (Pinkowski 1950). Rood (1898, 809) described the area as a "collection of shanties wherein exist the ten or eleven hundred foreign miners, with their few women and children." Hambidge noted that these houses reveal the "character" of the builder. He described an architectural asymmetry that existed among each of the shanty buildings. The roofs slanted at different angles. Some roofs had shingles, others had weatherboards, and others had rusty sheet iron. Some window openings were high and others were low. Some doors opened in and others opened out. The hinges and other hardware appeared to have been salvaged from the company scrap pile (Hambidge 1898, 824). Of flimsy construction, the houses had no plumbing or running water, and were not insulated from the elements (Pinkowski 1950, 6). Rood (1898, 818) noted in his racist tone, "As a rule, the foreigners in the anthracite fields have been content until recently to labor for very low wages without a protest; to huddle in shanties like so many domestic animals; to eat half-spoiled vegetables and fruits that could not be sold to English-speaking people." Hambidge (1898, 828) described the town as a scene of "despair, ignorance, strife, and struggle for mere existence."

All of the properties had fences. A local informant told us that the fences were not about keeping in animals. Rather, they were erected to keep animals out. The Italian section had predominantly goats and chickens, and the Slav section had geese and ducks. There are many local stories of goats roaming the streets, breaking through fences, and eating portions of neighbors' vegetable gardens. There are also stories of neighbors killing these goats when they invaded their property.

Recognition of the exact property boundaries was often not observed. Fence lines and outbuildings sometimes stood on adjacent properties. During the early settlement period the exact property boundaries meant very little to the original settlers, who worked long hours and simply needed shelter when they slept at night. Dog leg jogs in the property boundary lines exist today. They serve as a reminder of how these boundaries moved and were adjusted to accommodate existing buildings. Today, some of the boundaries' widths facing the street are thirty feet wide, whereas others are twenty-eight feet wide. Other property boundaries remain indistinguishable.

As a result of the Great Depression, the Lattimer Coal Company eventually sold the patch town to the Hazle Realty Company, which in turn sold the properties to the current tenants. At this time there was an attempt to redefine and "straighten out" some of the property boundaries. Right angles were created from the boundaries along the road. People began to contest the misplacement of fences and buildings on property (Roller 2015, 2018b). To this day, just about every landowner in Pardeesville discusses issues related to property boundary lines, and just about every landowner claims that they have more land than what their new deed indicates that they own.

The Italian village is situated on a slope, and it is obvious why the village was not part of the original planned community. During heavy rains, the area floods as water washes down the slope from the surrounding high areas. Many of the people who lived in the village have slowly moved from the area for various reasons. Some moved to "on top," a higher elevation that is generally flat and well drained. This is the modern section of Pardeesville, with many of the houses built in the 1960s and 1970s. Others moved to the larger city of Hazleton, or out of the region.

Several houses have been removed from the Italian village, while a few others stand vacant and condemned. Some of those residents who remain in the village area live at bare subsistence levels. One of the former residents told me how his family owned and lived in a nearby house. There was a leak in the roof and the family was too poor to repair the leak. Instead, the family moved to the first floor of the house. They lived there until the roof was so damaged that the house was condemned and they had to move to a relative's house in a nearby town. Some of the residents do not work, or have seasonal employment. Parts of the community barely subsist in the underground economy. Those who are employed on a regular basis tend to work in construction or drive several hours a day to work in the fracking industry.

During our summer excavations it became apparent why the Italian village was allocated to the poorest settlers of Pardeesville. There is no sewer system to capture the rain runoff. During our stay, a major summer rainstorm dropped three inches of rain and caused significant damage to some of the inhabited homes in the Italian village. Those who lived "on top" fared well in the deluge. However, those living in the lower-lying areas received the runoff from the slope, and houses were flooded. The south side of Church Street received a considerable amount of drainage from the slope runoff, and the ground surface held 1–1.5 feet of water for a short time before it was able to run off into the adjacent strip mine. These conditions demonstrated why houses no longer stood or were abandoned on these lots. The new Italian immigrant received some of the poorest land upon which to build their shanties.

Taking Control of Their Welfare

The early descriptions of Lattimer No. 2 indicate that the houses in the Italian village were constructed by individuals rather than the coal company, probably in the 1880s and 1890s. The archaeology of the first-generation domestic structures indicates that contiguous stone foundations do not exist for this early construction phase of the shantytown. It is likely that stones were used as piers and served as the foundation for the shanties, or the first shanty buildings were constructed without foundations. There are a few remaining frame structures built at the end of the nineteenth century in northeastern Pennsylvania with sills laying directly on the ground without foundations or piers.

In Lattimer No. 2, the archaeology revealed a jumble of stones that are related to the original settlement. There is also significant burning associated with this early layer dating to the late nineteenth century. Very few nails were found in this earliest burned layer. Therefore, it seems likely that these structures burned (either intentionally or by accident) and the nails were scavenged to be used elsewhere in subsequent construction projects.

The second-generation occupation of the village began in the early twentieth century, probably shortly after the *Century* magazine revealed the living conditions in this patch town. The occupants still paid land rent to the coal operators. A historic photograph with a house in the background and a few existing, abandoned buildings provide clues about the second generation of building. These homes along Church Street were more substantial than the original shanties. The archaeology uncovered a variety of foundation construction techniques that ranged from stone and concrete piers to continuously laid stone foundations that ranged from 1.0 to 2.5 feet deep. One of the houses had a poured concrete floor (Roller 2018a).

In 1940, the Lattimer Coal Company was losing considerable revenue as a result of the Great Depression and the general downturn of the coal industry. One of their strategies to help increase revenue was to dissolve the company of all of their land holdings. They sold the land that contained domestic houses to the Hazle Realty Company. At that point the Hazle Realty Company gave those who were occupying the houses the option to purchase their house and land. Some of those who then moved "on top" abandoned their houses, while others dismantled their homes and used the wood and nails to construct outbuildings and additions to their new domiciles "on top" (Roller 2018a).

From Corporate Control to Individual Ownership: The Gardens

While working in the Italian village, we noticed a long, rectangular depression that measured about twenty feet wide and thirty feet long and was about 1–1.5 feet below the surrounding surface. We wondered if it was a natural feature, or if it was created by the last occupants. A resident who is related to the former owner of the property noted that those in the Italian village spent significant time tending their gardens in their backyards. The entire backyards were planted, except for where outbuildings were located. They spent a lot of time ensuring that the soil was well maintained. They mixed coal ashes from their stoves into their gardens and then added some lime to counter the acidity of the coal. The careful mixing of the soil with the appropriate amount of coal ash, loam, and lime influenced the flavor of the vegetables grown in their gardens. In particular, this informant spoke about how important it was to get the correct soil mixture of coal ash and lime for good-tasting tomatoes. Starting in the 1940s, some of the long-time residents began to abandon the Italian village and moved "on top." They sought better living conditions that were also less congested. The newer sections of the town—"on top"—are located on a ridge line, the highest elevation in town. These new homes had larger lots and newer and more modern facilities. Some of the houses in the old section stood vacant and slowly decayed from the lack of maintenance. A few were eventually condemned and dismantled. The families that moved "on top" brought their furniture and other belongings to their new domiciles. Some families also moved the soil from their gardens in the village to the yards of their new homes. They valued the time and effort they had invested in creating their garden soil, creating vegetables that appealed to their taste, so it was important to bring the garden with them to their new homes, thus explaining the shallow rectangular depression. They would be ensured of quality vegetables that they had become accustomed to growing. This phenomenon, the moving of garden soil, occurred throughout the old section of Pardeesville as families moved "on top."

Our informant lived in Lattimer No. 2 (now Pardeesville) for over seventy years. He spent a portion of his life in the older section of Lattimer No. 2—the Italian village. He came to the archaeology site several times a week and reminisced about growing up in Lattimer No. 2. He told us about how hard his mother worked keeping house and doing household chores all day. It was also necessary for her to work in the garden, because a successful garden could supply vegetables for the family through the lean times of the year. He told us that one morning while his mother worked in their garden in the 1930s, she lost her wedding band. In the 1950s the family moved "on top," and like some of the other residents, they took their garden soil with them. About two decades later, our informant found the wedding band in the soil in the yard of the new house as he was gardening.

Landscape and Garden in the Slavic Community

We excavated in another backyard in the planned Slavic community of Lattimer No. 2. Based on old maps, the Yanac house was constructed around 1870. It is part of a set of double houses that line Lower Street and Upper Street only a short distance from the Italian village. Hambidge (1898, 824) described these houses thus: "The regular company house is a square structure built of raw lumber, which the weather and coal-dust have stained a dirty brown, and which from a distance takes a general tone of black, relieved only by the clear sky above. The fences about the little plots of ground attached to each house are constructed in a haphazard way." These houses were originally constructed two rooms deep with a detached kitchen and a privy.

Families rented these houses from the company, and the occupants constructed outbuildings in the backyards and used the remaining land for gardening. Eventually the kitchens were attached with a hyphen. Therefore, the typical double house in the coal region today consists of a main block, a hyphen, and an attached kitchen. In Lattimer No. 2, by the 1940s, privies were replaced with cesspools and wildcat sewers.

The yard spaces were economized, and oral histories indicate that almost every square foot of the yard that did not have an outbuilding was usually planted with vegetables. The workers' gardens were about economy and raising enough food for the family. The current landscape at the Yanac house has three terraces, with the third and highest terrace being the farthest away from the house and the first terrace containing the house. The terracing of this yard space is unique to the area. Most of the yards in town are either at an even elevation (south side of Lower Street), or if they are on the hillside (like the north side of Lower Street, and the properties along Upper Street), they have sloped backyards.

Determining when the terraces were constructed provides us with clues about how the space was utilized and shows how the residents maximized their space, especially in times of tough economic situations. The first terrace at the house was graded in the early twenty-first century in order to keep eroding soils away from the house. Therefore, we did not place any excavation units on this terrace. Archaeological excavations on the second terrace indicate that there is a clear signature of a buried A horizon, meaning a previous ground surface that was probably used for gardening. The archaeology shows that there is a natural slope in the yard, with the high point in the west and decreasing in elevation in the east portion of the yard. The topography also dramatically slopes from the north end to the south end. There is some erosion from the second and third terraces toward the first terrace, giving a slight sloping grade to the yard surface.

The dominant narrative of coal country is that every usable space in the yard was used for gardens, especially since the men were paid a meager wage and they often did not work a full week, either because of decreasing coal consumption, especially during the summers, or because of occasional work stoppages. In several of the excavation units it is clear that shovel divots are in the subsoil, a signature that gardening was performed in the backyards. Wall profiles of the excavation units also show signs of digging slightly into the subsoil.

Gardening is a very important part of the economy of coal communities. There are references to families taking extra care to prepare their gardens in anticipation of a long strike. Based on the archaeological analysis, it appears that the terracing occurred sometime in the early twentieth century. Terracing was one way to prevent erosion on the slopes from impacting the garden after a very heavy rain episode. While gardening occurred on each of the terraces, it is plausible that the terraces were constructed in anticipation of a strike to ensure maximum garden yield.

There is evidence of food preservation, as canning jar lids indicate that the occupants were preserving vegetables for the long term—a way to "make ends meet." Part of the local narrative is that women were responsible for planting and keeping the garden in addition to being responsible for the household. Many of the women also held wage-paying jobs in Hazleton, mostly in the textile factory (Westmont 2019).

As residents gained some independence from the coal company and families began finding steady and better-paying employment elsewhere, their households could rely on larger commercial markets, which also meant a decreasing reliance on their vegetable gardens. Photographs from the late 1940s show how the use of the backyard space changed significantly. The vegetable gardens were transformed into an ornamental space. Grasses replaced vegetables, and shrubs lined the edges of terraces. While the signature of survival for the coal miners was the garden, this landscape feature faded, as did the memory of the men and women of the coal patch towns.

Sanitation

Sanitation was a serious problem, especially for those who lived in the Italian village. Dogs, pigs, and goats roamed the alleys. Hambidge (1898, 824), writer and illustrator for the *Century* magazine, explained that Lattimer No. 2 did not have a sewage system, and the alleys served as the receptacle for kitchen and human waste. Hambidge explained, "There is no sewage system, and the alley is the dumping-ground for all offal. At every few steps of this winding, reeking way are little openings leading into other passageways, not much wider than will permit a man to walk through" (1898, 824).

The poor sanitation affected the infant mortality rate in these communities. Peter Roberts ([1904] 1970, 79) wrote, "Better sanitary conditions ought to prevail, and if the Christian people of these communities who bewail the slaughter of infants of Bethlehem were to arouse themselves to the slaughter of the innocents which goes on annually in anthracite mining towns, better conditions would soon prevail and a moiety of the suffering and loss would be mitigated." He later described the stench as a result of the poor sanitary conditions. "The offal, the dish-water, the suds from the washing, and even the excretions of the human body were thrown from the door or window of the dwelling, and all this filth in the glare of the summer's sun, gave rise to the effluvia that was sickening. What wonder is there that under such conditions the death-rate of the slums is found here on the mountain heights?" (Roberts [1904] 1970, 132). The child mortality rate tended to be much higher in these patch towns. Diseases such as measles and typhoid ran rampant in these communities. In some mining communities, as many as 40 percent of the children died before they made it to adolescence (Bodnar 1982; Miller and Sharpless 1998, 195; Roberts [1904] 1970).

The waste water from households was not a concern of the coal operator, however after the first generation of settlement, efforts were often made by individuals to improve sanitary conditions. One remedy to improve sanitation was to construct cesspools. In the early twentieth century, wood-lined cesspools were created in the backyards of Lattimer No. 2. A typical cesspool is a hole several feet in diameter and several feet deep. It is usually constructed of a porous material that allows for liquids to seep through, although strong enough to keep the structure from collapsing. While the waste flowed into the top of the chamber, the solids decayed and collected as composted matter in the base of the cesspool. The raw sewage entered the groundwater with minimal biological cleansing, leading to groundwater contamination, which impacted drinking wells. Ideally, cesspools should be downhill and five hundred feet away from wells or springs used for drinking water. The cesspools in the Italian village were vulnerable to overloading or overflowing caused by heavy rains or snowmelt because they were not sealed like contemporary conventional septic tank systems.

We discovered a wood-lined cesspool about one and a half feet below the surface and about one hundred feet to the rear of the domicile. As the feature was exposed at the surface, it measured about five by five feet square and was about five feet deep (Illustration 2.1). The bottom of the feature was on a solid clay and stone layer. Each wall had two horizontal boards at the base of the cesspool for the lowest foot of the feature, with vertical boards resting on the horizontal boards for the remaining four feet of the feature. The feature was mostly filled with stone rubble, probably from the demolition of the house in the early 1960s. Most of the artifacts found in the feature are related to the filling of the cesspool and date from the 1940s through the 1950s.

Oral histories indicate that the decayed matter from privies and cesspools was used as fertilizer and spread throughout the backyards to enrich the soils for the gardens. The cesspool on this property was cleaned out before it was filled with construction rubble. Its content was probably used as fertilizer. Less than an inch of organic matter, filled with seeds, was located at the base of the feature.

The cesspool in this backyard was at a higher elevation than several of the houses located on nearby adjacent lots. There is a strong likelihood that effluence may have contaminated the drinking water of these adjacent houses, especially during times of heavy rain and large snowmelts. After the coal company sold the properties to the Hazle Realty Company, which in turn sold them to the residents, a new sanitation method was created in the form of wildcat sewer systems. The initial investment was costlier than the cesspool system, although, in the long term, it also meant that the chances for groundwater contamination decreased significantly.

Archaeological excavations uncovered a four-inch metal pipe adjacent to and parallel to a second-generation house in the Italian village. Much like Hambidge (1898) described regarding the first-generation occupation in the late nineteenth century, the pipe for the second-generation house ran directly into the alley adjacent to the house. The pipe was close to the surface, and it appears that while it carried gray water away from the

Illustration 2.1. Locating the cesspool in the rear of a lot in Pardeesville, Pennsylvania. Image by Paul A. Shackel.

house and toward to the alley, gravity was also necessary to carry the water downhill and toward Upper Street. This piping of gray water probably continued until the abandonment of the house in the 1950s. This alley is the one described in the *Century* magazine as filled with waste and malodorous. It continued to carry effluence for another half a century.

To remedy the waste water found in alleys, communities constructed wildcat sewer systems. The wildcat sewer system collects waste water and raw sewage and discharges it into ditches, streams, rivers, or abandoned mines. Some coal operators built sophisticated bore holes and sewage pipe systems that carried sewage away from domestic areas (Learn 1994). Wildcat sewers were common in Lattimer No. 2 and placed throughout the town, although not until the Lattimer Coal Company relinquished control of their residential lands. One of the older town residents remembers digging ditches for these wildcat sewer lines around 1941. When families purchased their houses and became responsible for their own welfare, they took control of their health and sanitation situation. The community built wildcat sewers to alleviate the sanitation problem. These wildcat sewage systems are not processed through a treatment plant, however. People who drink water from rivers and streams with raw sewage have a high potential of contracting salmonella or shigella bacteria. These bacteria can cause diarrhea, vomiting, and, in rare cases, death. The sewage also consumes oxygen in water, which, in turn, impacts wildlife (Learn 1994). Wildcat sewers still exist in some northeastern Pennsylvania communities. While they are now illegal, they are sometimes difficult to detect. They are also difficult to eliminate because of the high cost of connecting households to a public sewer system. The wildcat system usually affects the poorest members of the community (Ragan 2011).

We found terracotta pipe fragments throughout the entire site of Lattimer No. 2. Apparently, the older terracotta pipes, which were placed in the ground, three feet deep, in 1941, were replaced with a clay pipe system in the 1970s. The clay pipes were manufactured by the Robinson Pottery Company in Pottstown, Pennsylvania, which manufactured clay pipes until 1995. Construction drawings dating to 1982 for Hazle Township show the development of a public sewer system with the use of PVC pipes running down the streets and connecting to the town's houses. The community also constructed a water tank to supply fresh spring water to the entire town.

Conclusion

The racialization of the new immigrants arriving in the anthracite coal region left the newcomers in a difficult position. Coal operators did not think it inappropriate to provide the new immigrants with substandard housing, and sometimes no housing at all. While the coal operators did little to address the housing needs for the new workers, they also did not pay attention to the poor sanitation conditions that were prevalent in the Lattimer communities, as well as throughout the anthracite region. Gardens were also developed by households in order to ensure that families had enough food during lean times. While these communities coped with these deprivations in housing, hygiene, and subsistence, as well as a toxified environment, the material evidence also helps develop the foundation for understanding the current deprivations in the health and well-being in the region today. The racialization of the new immigrant population over a century ago justified these conditions and led to a form of structural violence that impacts the present-day community.

CHAPTER 3

Historic Trauma
Health and Well-Being in Northeastern Pennsylvania

Structural Violence in Northeastern Pennsylvania

Understanding the long-term impact of social and economic inequalities is an important part of our work in northeastern Pennsylvania. The poor general health and well-being in this region has deeper roots: a history of exploitation of new immigrants, the spoiling and toxification of the environment, and the general poor support for the new population's general health and well-being. A historical perspective examining the long-term trauma and structural violence provides a vehicle for understanding the general poor health and well-being of the contemporary population.

There is a growing literature that shows that historical trauma can impact a community's health and well-being, especially in relation to racial and ethnic minority populations (Mohatt and Tebes 2014). Historical trauma (also known as transgenerational trauma, and intergenerational trauma) was first noticed in the 1960s, when researchers described the symptoms experienced by descendants of Holocaust survivors (Phipps and Degges-White 2014). Brave Heart (1999) extended this work to show how historical trauma impacted American Indian groups. Subsequent studies have shown the impact on other ethnic and minority groups that have faced racism and discrimination (Mims et al. 2001).

Generally, historical trauma is the result of negative health and well-being conditions associated with cumulative group trauma across generations. Trauma responses include elevated mortality rates and health problems emanating from heart disease, hypertension, alcohol abuse, and suicidal behavior (Brave Heart 1999, 2003). Historical trauma theory relies on the premise that populations historically subjected to long-term, mass trauma, such as colonialism, slavery, war, and genocide, as well as everyday experiences of discrimination and racism, will exhibit a higher prevalence of disease, even when these descendants do not have direct experience of the trauma (Evans-Campbell 2008; Michaels et al. 2010; Sotero 2006). The trauma is transmitted over generations.

   The new immigrants who came to the anthracite region, as well as subsequent generations, tended to be malnourished and sometimes close to starvation. Studies indicate that when there are challenges to mental health, and when populations are faced with malnutrition, the impact on subsequent generations' health and well-being increases (Devakumar et al. 2014). R. M. Phipps and S. Degges-White (2014) have shown the impact of trauma on immigrant groups, who face discrimination, psychological abuse, and malnutrition. Such research demonstrates how a deteriorating environment, which poses significant health threats, and the continuous threat of starvation affected the general health and well-being of northeastern Pennsylvania communities over a century ago, and how this trauma may be impacting the general health and well-being of these communities today (Shackel 2018c).

   The substandard health and well-being found in contemporary northeastern Pennsylvania may be in part due to the transgenerational result of the structural violence encountered by new immigrants from Southern and Eastern Europe a century ago, as they were racialized and exploited for many subsequent generations. Johan Galtung (1969, 1990) notes that structural violence is embedded in social institutions and structures of oppression, such as racism, sexism, homophobia, and elitism, that do harm by preventing people from meeting their basic needs. Structural violence is difficult to see. Because structural violence is avoidable, it is a high cause of premature death and unnecessary illnesses and disability (Little and Shackel 2014). Following are some of the forms of historical trauma and long-term structural violence that have impacted this region and have culminated in northeastern Pennsylvania being labeled the unhappiest place to live in the United States.

Forms of Historical Trauma and Long-Term Structural Violence in Northeastern Pennsylvania

Long-Term Impact on Landscape and Environment

The long-term degradation of the environment as a result of anthracite mining has impacted and continues to impact the people of northeastern Pennsylvania. In general, nonwhite and low-income people have, for a long time, been disproportionately exposed to environmental hazards

(Pulido 1996, 142). The trauma from the exploitation of workers, and the disregard for their health and well-being, is evident on the landscape and remains a haunting problem in today's descendant community as they try to eke out a livelihood in a region that is now well-known for deindustrialization (Shackel 2018c).

The impact of mining in the anthracite region was devastating from the very beginning of the coal extraction industry. As early as 1866, a guidebook writer questioned the benefits of coal and the impact on the landscape. "Improvements unquestionably have been made, and great ones too; but why, in carrying them out, it should be necessary to mar (and it would seem to have been done almost wantonly in many instances) the face of nature by stripping the hill and mountain-side of the growth and grove of trees . . . doth give us pause" (quoted in Goin and Raymond 2001, 31).

Culm banks developed throughout the region; these are piles, hills, and small mountain-like rounded features that are found near breakers. Culm is a derivative from Middle English or Welsh, the ethnicity of the first miners in the region, and refers to coal mine waste or inferior anthracite, and includes rock, soil, and small pieces of coal too small to sell. (Other regions refer to these waste piles as tailings, gob piles, slate dumps, or boney piles.) While these culm banks are large, they represent about 50 percent of the material extracted from the ground. The other 50 percent is the coal that has been shipped out of the region. In 1869, a Dr. Holister wrote, "The eruptions of culm piles, heightened into pyramids, all formed of the purest coal, around every breaker from Carbondale to Nanticoke, exhibit the certainty and rapidity with which our streams are being choked and our mountains turned wrong side out by a process alike exhausting and wasteful. It offers its advantage to the indolent consumer, but how fatal to the interior and exterior of our unresisting hills and valleys" (quoted in Stevenson 1931, 72). In 1898 Henry Edward Rood, writing for the *Century* magazine, described a scene in the coal patch town of Lattimer:

> The level land between the culm and the hillside whereon the foreigners live is devoid of vegetation. Grasses and wild flowers once were luxuriant there, but for many decades rains have been washing from the huge pile some of the deadly black particles that smother plants, even trees, as we realize by noting the gaunt, leafless, lifeless trunks scattered here and there, with naked grayish limbs uplifted as if crying to Heaven for help. Were it not for the green hillsides and the kaleidoscopic sky, this would be indeed a somber picture. To the immigrant just arrived from Italy the colliery town must seem a realization of desolation itself. (Rood 1898, 809)

By the early twentieth century, studies began documenting the living conditions of the new immigrants. Sociologist Peter Roberts's book, *Anthracite Coal Communities* ([1904] 1970), condemns the coal industry for destroying the landscape and the environment. He commented on the changing landscape and described the by-product of several generations of mining and environmental degradation: "A great change has come over this charming landscape. . . . But in nothing is the change so marked as in the character of these mountain streams. . . . Now the rain and snow have no natural reservoirs. . . . Every storm means a flood. . . . The mining industry perfects the work of destruction" (Roberts [1904] 1970, 6). Later in his book he described:

> The contamination of our streams, the black creeks full of water laden with coal-dust, the dismal acres where the refuse from washeries has long been turned—these make a dreary environment. Trunks of trees stand in the valley, veritable ghosts of stately pines which no more know spring-time and summer. In many places acres of culm heaps, which are the refuse of a century of mining, stand as black monsters defiling our fairest valleys; the huge black breakers and shafts enveloped in a cloud of smoke and steam and dust when in operations; the scores of mining patches where houses have been built with depressing uniformity, while around them are the heaps of ashes, tin-cans, old bottles, empty beer kegs, etc. (Roberts [1904] 1970, 155)

Abandoned deep mines continue to have a long-term impact on water resources in the region. Today, the Commonwealth of Pennsylvania has more than 250,000 acres of abandoned mine lands, a total that is higher than in any other state. These abandoned mines have also impacted five thousand miles of waterways from pollution and acid mine drainage (AMD) (Earth Conservancy 2017; Zawacki 2015). It is common to see streams and rivers flowing with different-colored water, with orange being the predominant color. In 2000, one resident described Panther Creek, which feeds into the Little Schuylkill: "I've seen it black, green, orange—almost like an orange oxide color. I've seen it purple. I've seen it red. I've never seen it clear" (quoted in Mailer 2000) (Illustration 3.1).

While deep mining sometimes occurred under the natural water table, the water naturally finds its way to the lowest point, the deepest point of the mine. Mine operations used pumps to keep the water from flooding the mines, a costly operation. When deep mining ceased throughout the anthracite region and the pumps stopped, the mines filled with water, mixing and reacting with the coal, and filling streets, basements, and streams with polluted mine water. The *New York Times* reported as early as 1924 the condition of some of the abandoned mines and described how they were filled with water. As a result of this flooding, the federal

Illustration 3.1. Abandoned mine filled with acid mine drainage. High quantities of iron oxide from mine runoff have changed the water's pH and made this water lifeless. Image by Paul A. Shackel.

government drilled boreholes in the abandoned mines to prevent the mine water from destroying property. Now, the majority of the mine water drains into waterways, creating another environmental disaster, known as acid mine drainage (AMD), sometimes referred to as abandoned mine drainage, or most recently as acid rock drainage (ARD). To complicate matters, for a long time chemical waste such as dichlorobenzene was illegally dumped into abandoned mines, impacting the nearby streams and rivers and contaminating the drinking water (Miller and Sharpless 1981, 176–77; Shackel 2017).

Generally, the term AMD refers to the low pH found in waters draining from active and abandoned mines. Sulfides in the rocks react with water and oxygen to form sulfuric acid and iron oxide. These waters also carry heavy metals, such as iron, aluminum, arsenic, and lead, to nearby streams. In the northern fields, most of the AMD discharges have a heavy concentration of iron, with a pH around 6.5. In the middle and southern fields, the discharges are more acidic, at a pH of 4.0, with heavy concentrations of aluminum (Zawacki 2015). The runoff is sometimes visible, as streams and rivers with a high level of iron oxide turn an orange color. The cloudiness of the water inhibits sunlight from penetrating, therefore prohibiting photosynthesis, thereby damaging the lowest level of the food chain. In some cases, the heavy metal runoff is not detectable. The high acid content not only kills wildlife; it also impacts structures built in water and can dissolve bridge piers (Marsh 1987). In order to address AMD, water discharge from mines is usually held in ponds until it can be treated and neutralized, which also allows sediments to sink to the bottom of the pond. The United States Geological Survey (USGS) recommends that acidic water produced at active mines be neutralized to between pH 6–9 before being discharged to a stream (USGS 2017).

AMD can occur naturally, but its impact becomes heightened with large-scale earth disturbances, such as construction sites, subdivisions, and transportation corridors, in areas where rocks contain sulfide minerals. In areas where there is drainage from culm banks and coal washeries the water drainage is highly acidic, and iron, manganese, sulfur, mercury, and aluminum can leach into nearby streams and waterways (Ewall, 2017). AMD also may be detectable in the winter, since mine water is a constant 55 degrees Fahrenheit, thus allowing streams impacted by AMD to flow during the winter freeze. Neutral mine drainage occurs when the water flow from the mine is not acidic, being neutralized along its flow. However, it can contain dissolved metals or metalloids.

The Jeddo Tunnel was constructed over three years and completed in 1894 at a cost of about $1 million. When completed, the five-mile tunnel was hailed as a major engineering feat and was the largest mine drainage tunnel in the world. While mining is mostly defunct in the area, the tunnel still drains an average of 40,000 gallons of water per minute, and at times up to 100,000 gallons per minute. The average pH of the Jeddo Tunnel drainage is 4.3. More than 90,000 pounds (41,000 kilograms) of acid drain from the Jeddo Tunnel into the Susquehanna River (via Little Nescopeck and Nescopeck Creeks) every day. An average of 2,900 pounds (1,300 kilograms) of aluminum, 1,350 pounds (610 kilograms) of manganese, and 860 pounds (390 kilograms) of iron flow from the Jeddo Tunnel each day (*Coal Age* 1914, 391; Mendinsky and Dempsey 2004; Shackel 2017).

The *Times Tribune* (2016) reported that Pennsylvania needs many billions of dollars in mine reclamation work at hundreds of sites to remedy physically dangerous and toxic landscapes. In 2015, the Pennsylvania Department of Environmental Protection awarded $52 million for reclamation projects statewide, which included several million dollars in Luzerne County, where Lattimer is located. However, the reclamation depends on a tax on current mining, so the decline in mining there will result in a decline in reclamation funding.

One successful nonprofit group addressing the environmental degradation as a result of mining is the Earth Conservancy. Beginning in 1992, the organization was able to establish a program to purchase

16,300 acres of mined land once belonging to the bankrupt Blue Coal Corporation in Ashley, Pennsylvania. The communities impacted by the company's mining are located only a few miles west of Wilkes-Barre. The Earth Conservancy is dedicated to reclamation, conservation, and economic revitalization of the mined landscape in northeastern Pennsylvania. The organization obtained a grant for $14 million and secured an additional $2 million in private loans in 1994 to return the lands to productive use. To date, the Earth Conservancy has reclaimed nearly 2,000 of its 16,300 acres at a cost of $42.8 million (Earth Conservancy 2017; Shackel 2017). The reclamation work still has a long way to go and will take a strong and continuous effort by the community for generations to come.

Subsidence

Families living in the anthracite region continuously fear losing their houses, not necessarily because of mortgage foreclosures, but rather because of land subsidence. As a result of underground mining, subsidence has been an issue in the anthracite region for well over a century. Sinkholes can occur without any warning, and they are scattered throughout the landscape. Some are more noticeable than others, and some have had significant impacts on the landscape, with very tragic outcomes. The most famous and well-commemorated subsidence event is the Stockton Mine disaster. The Stockton Mine subsidence occurred at 5:00 a.m. on 18 December 1869 and claimed ten lives. Active mining was underway beneath a residential area in Stockton, a town close to Hazleton, when two houses were swallowed into the ground, falling forty feet and killing all of those inside the dwellings. A third home went into the subsidence as well, although those who were in the house eventually escaped (*New York Times* 1869a, 1869b). Today, at the disaster site, there is a stone memorial surrounded by a fence, and a wooden sign commemorating the event. Two days later, 20 December 1869, the *New York Times* reported that in Mauch Chunk, which is now called Jim Thorpe, "One block of houses were swallowed up in the cavity so quickly that two families living in them had not time to escape" (*New York Times* 1869a). Apparently, the mining in this event had occurred within only twenty feet of the surface, which caused the subsidence.

Subsidence events still occur throughout the region. Roads are sometimes in disrepair because of subsidence. Usable building sites are rare. In some places structures lean, and they give way to subsidence activities. "Structures slowly settle and pitch, and frame buildings lean precariously toward the road, waiting for the owners to adjust the house jacks to this month's topography" (Marsh 1987, 347). The degree of subsidence depends on several factors; some or all can come into play to undermine the earth to create subsidence. First, it depends on the amount of coal extracted, the thickness of the coal veins, and the strength of the rock strata between the coal veins. As mines fill with water and the water interacts with the submerged soft rock, it undermines the remaining rock. Second, when mines were being abandoned the remaining coal that served as support pillars was "robbed," thereby creating a weaker roof structure. Third, timbers, used for supporting roofs and walls, eventually rot and collapse, leaving the former mines more vulnerable to collapse (Miller and Sharpless 1981, 177). There are more than a million homes in Pennsylvania that sit on top of abandoned coal mines, and they may succumb to subsidence without warning at any time (Gallo 2017).

Long-Term Impact of Coal Contamination

Coal contains sulfur and other elements, such as mercury, lead, and arsenic. When it is burned, these and other elements are released into the atmosphere. Large amounts of carbon dioxide (CO_2) are also released, which increases the greenhouse effect in the atmosphere. There are several innovations being developed to make coal burn cleaner. Integrated gasification combined cycle (IGCC) technology converts coal into gas and removes sulfur and metals. The gas generates electricity while sulfur and metals are collected, and eventually sold. This technology is now being developed to capture CO_2 emissions. Another technology, carbon sequestration, helps to capture and store carbon underground rather than releasing it into the atmosphere. Some coal-burning plants store the carbon in abandoned underground mines, while others pump the carbon into sedimentary rocks or below the ocean floor.

    I have been to places in Luzerne County where residents have shown me how pollution from coal mining affects the daily lives of people living in patch towns next to active mining. While a few coal mining operations remain open, the prosperity for a few has meant environmental and health problems for many others. In late June and early July 2012, many of the residents in the coal patch town of Lattimer became quite vocal about the dust particles in the air as a result of quarrying and coal mining. White houses were becoming a bit grayer as coal dust settled on domiciles throughout the patch town. People also noticed a fine black residue on cars, as well as in swimming pool filters. One resident told me that she power washed her house a few months previously. Then she wiped her finger across the windowsill and left a streak behind. Her finger was blackened. This residue was not pollen or dust. It does not clean easily with just water, as it leaves a greasy film. Only a chemical wash will get it clean, although the formula is harmful to the surrounding vegetation and the water table. Some residents were spending more time indoors because of the new pollution. Some were complaining about allergy-like symptoms—sore throats and/or running nose. Some of the town's elderly complained about respiratory problems.

On 9 July 2012, Hazle Township residents met with mine supervisors and asked for help to mitigate the dust and noise coming from the quarrying activities. Residents complained that calls to the state Department of Environmental Protection did not generate results. According to reports in the local newspaper, the *Standard Speaker*, the governor's office and the state senator and state representative have deflected concerns to the Hazle Township officials. The Department of Environmental Protection asked residents to photograph dust plumes to prove the mine operations are causing problems. One resident noted that a photograph was taken of a dust plume near the coal operations. The resident observed that he would have thought that he had photographed a brush fire had he not been aware of the quarry operations (Galski 2012, A5).

The Pennsylvania Department of Environmental Protection performed two years of air quality monitoring. The levels of dust monitored at four locations were between 3.53 tons per square mile and 5.05 tons per square mile. The air quality standards recommend that dust levels at or above 4.3 tons per square mile require air quality controls. However, the company was only told to work on minimizing dust from their operations (Rowland 2015). Interestingly, a few community members stated to me that they believe that the company has a right to make a profit, and they were reluctant to get the government involved. However, the community is not happy with the company, and their anger is amplified because they feel the Commonwealth of Pennsylvania and local government have not provided adequate environmental protection for their community. People feel that they are fighting big corporations and a government agency that is siding with the mining companies (Shackel 2016).

What is happening to the residents of Hazle Township is a microcosm of a larger problem associated with the coal industry. After decades of decline, black lung disease is back with a vengeance. Its resurgence is concentrated in central Appalachia, although miners from other regions are prone to getting the disease. There are many recorded infractions and air quality samples showing that miners have been exposed to more dust than is allowed by the federal Mine Safety and Health Administration (MSHA). Elected officials—including those representing the affected areas by the disease—are quick to embrace the industry while being slow to address its larger impacts (Bump 2012).

Coal was king in the anthracite region for well over a century, and it still holds power in the region. When driving through the region, there are many pro-coal roadside advertisements, and the coal companies tout the benefits of coal extraction. Blaschak Coal Company operates in the anthracite region. The company website notes several benefits to using anthracite coal. They note that one reason for using anthracite coal is that it is produced in the United States by American workers. Unlike oil and gas, its availability and pricing are not subject to international policy (Blaschak Coal Company 2017).

Long-Term Impact of Nutritional Deprivation

Long-term deprivations in living and working conditions and deficiencies in nutrition among the region's traditional population can be documented from the late nineteenth century through oral histories documentary research and archaeology. This information shows that malnutrition may have led to the transgenerational effects of poor health and general unhappiness that continues to affect the contemporary descendant community of the Southern and Eastern European immigrants to the area. For instance, one informant from the anthracite region described living conditions in a coal patch town during the 1930s and 1940s, explaining that,

> [When I was young we] had a little garden. One summer, that is all we ate, what was growing in the garden. I ate a lot of green apples and plums from my neighbor's trees. During the summer we couldn't even wait until they got ripe; we start eating them. . . . I was even deprived of milk. Don't touch it. I even said to my mother, "Why can't I drink the milk?" "Because that is for your father. He's the one that works; he's the one that has to eat." We were pretty poor. (Quoted in Dublin 1998, 73)

The archaeology at several coal patch towns provides a glimpse of the health and nutrition of the historic populations. For instance, at Eckley, the archaeology project focused on structures found on Back Street, an area that contained the smallest domestic structures in town that were initially inhabited by the newest immigrants. The men were generally laborers and occupied the lowest end of the work hierarchy, while the women maintained the household, catered to the needs of boarders, and maintained the household's gardens. At one site a total of thirteen excavation units were placed in the side and backyard areas of a double house. While 6,487 artifacts were recovered, only 195 faunal specimens were identified, which is relatively small in proportion to the entire assemblage.[1] The materials are highly fragmented, although bird, mammals, and mollusk are present. The mammals include cattle, sheep/goat, and white-tail deer. The cuts of beef are the most common identifiable portion of the assemblage and tend to be chuck primal cut, which is a low-quality cut and relatively inexpensive. It is usually ground for stews or dishes like *holubky* (see below). There are also several cow cranial fragments in the assemblage, suggesting the consumption of cow's head soup. The cow's skull is one of the cheapest meat products, yet when boiled over several hours its product is rich in protein, and it becomes the basis for a bone soup/broth. The sheep/goat remains are predominantly from the animals' hind foot. This shank cut is a lower quality and therefore cheaper to purchase. Chicken is the only identified bird bone. A tibia fragment from a white-tail deer indicates that hunting was necessary to supplement the family's diet (Shackel 2018c; Westmont 2017).

Another patch town, Lattimer No. 1, known today as Lattimer Mines, about six miles west of Eckley, developed in 1869. By the 1880s, the new immigrants from Southern and Eastern Europe began arriving to work as laborers in the Lattimer Mines. They were provided a parcel of land, rather than housing, and the newcomers constructed their own quarters (Roller 2015, 2018b; Shackel 2018a; Shackel and Roller 2012). Of twelve test units, five test units were placed in and around the summer kitchen, where no faunal remains were encountered, except for one pig's tusk. The tusk is in the shape of a horn and may have been used to ward off the evil eye (*malocchio, maloik*). Using horns (usually pig's tusk) to ward off evil spirits continues to be a common practice in the area among households of Italian descent, where they are usually placed near windows and doors. Shovel divots into the subsoil are a clear indication that gardening occurred in the backyard areas. Interviews with long-term residents confirm that the back areas were used primarily for gardening, and households tended to grow potatoes, cabbage, onions, beans, tomatoes, and squash (Roller 2015; Shackel 2016). These gardens had to supplement butcher-purchased meats and help sustain the family.

In general, the laborers' families living in these two coal patch towns probably struggled to maintain a high-protein diet necessary for difficult working conditions. They were always on the verge of starvation, because of unemployment, underemployment, or participation in strikes protesting unfair labor conditions; a few strikes lasted as long as six months. If protein did exist it tended to come from low-quality cuts of meat, or preserved meats like ground beef and sausage. Corroborating evidence from oral histories and other historical sources indicate that these communities mostly relied on vegetables and starches for the everyday diet of laborers and their families. A review of contemporary cookbooks dating to the early twentieth century provides another glimpse into the diet of the new immigrant, in this case people from Eastern Europe, and in particular, the Slovak community (Shackel 2018c).

The earliest printed cookbooks catering to Slovak cuisine in this region were published in the early twentieth century in the largest urban centers in the anthracite region, Scranton and Wilkes-Barre. They were printed at least one generation after the initial, large immigration from Southern and Eastern Europe. Many of these books were composed of gathered recipes, and their publication was sponsored by different social or church groups. Several cookbooks from the region survive; they contain a wide variety of dishes, ranging from meat preparation to traditional foods, including breads and pastries. In most of the cookbooks, the meat (beef, pork, and chicken) recipes consist on average of 5 percent of the entire cookbook. The preponderance of recipes tend to favor high-starch dishes (like potato pancakes, potato cakes, and dumplings filled with potato or cabbage, the latter which we know as *pierogi*, and *halušky*, consisting of a soft noodle or dumpling mixed with cabbage), and if protein is part of the recipe, it usually incorporates lower-quality cuts of meat, like ground beef (like *holubky*, also referred to as stuffed cabbage) and pigs' feet (like *studenina*, or jellied pig's feet) (First Catholic Slovak Ladies Union 1952; Langer 1975; McHale 1913; Woman's Institute of Domestic Arts and Sciences 1923; Wyoming Valley Women's Club 1925).

Cookbooks provide an important source for understanding the general diet and nutrition for part of the northeastern Pennsylvania community. While the diet may have changed somewhat from the time of the initial immigration to the development of the recipes found in these cookbooks, this source provides some insight into the community's access or lack of access to a high-protein diet. They relied extensively on vegetables and starch. While the faunal assemblage produces few remains, they did rely on processed meats for special occasions (Shackel 2018c).

In Lattimer No. 2, the Anthracite Heritage Project excavated a 1960s assemblage. Recovered artifacts include items like light bulbs, tableware, and nail polish containers, among many other familiar, contemporary material culture items. There are also large quantities of over-the-counter medicinal bottles/containers in the assemblage, such as Bayer aspirin, Noxzema cream, and a bottle fragment with the embossed: "HAND MED CO."/ "PHILADELPHIA." There are several eye droppers, as well as many unidentified medicine vials and other medicine containers. Also included in the assemblage are a dozen hypodermic needles used for insulin shots to treat diabetes. According to a local interviewee, the resident that occupied the house, who was of Slovak ancestry, struggled with diabetes and the disease was eventually the cause of his death. While the standard of living in these coal patch towns improved for some, poor health conditions were prevalent in this particular household, and they may be linked to the long-term structural violence that perpetuated social, political, and economic inequities and health disparities (Shackel 2018c).

Poverty and Depopulation

Barry Bluestone and Bennett Harrison (1982, 12) describe the fundamental struggle between capital and community, quoting planning theorist John Friedman: "The capitalist city has no reverence for life. It bulldozes over neighborhoods to make way for business. It abandons entire regions, because profits are greater somewhere else. Deprived of their life spaces, people's lives are reduced to a purely economic dimension as workers and consumers—so long, at least, as there is work" (Freidman, quoted in Bluestone and Harrison 1982, 47). Instead of providing new employment opportunities, a higher standard of living, and enhanced security, the decision of capitalism to abandon the anthracite coal region has resulted in the opposite—fewer employment opportunities, a comparatively lower standard of living, and decreased security (Shackel and Westmont 2016).

As a result, towns in the anthracite region are being depopulated at an alarming rate, by some estimates 10 percent per decade starting in the 1970s (Marsh 1987). It is common to see abandoned houses and boarded-up storefronts throughout the region. Some towns have a higher vacancy rate than others. One news report described these communities as ghost towns, as some of them have or are approaching a 25 percent vacancy rate for homes and businesses. People are leaving these towns and abandoning their homes and businesses without selling them. Because of the high vacancy rate, many of the homes for sale in these communities sell for less than $15,000 (Bohman 2012).

Even with its shrinking population and high vacancy rate, some towns have a resurgence of visitors for a day or two each year. For instance, the town of Shenandoah is home to an annual kielbasa festival that draws about seven thousand people, mostly from the local region. The streets fill with vendors selling food and Eastern European crafts. However, the following day the streets are once again empty, with vacant houses and vacant storefronts. A real estate agent explained the town's situation: "It's a great little town, but it has an image problem. . . . I've brought people up here to show them downtown properties as far as commercial, and the comment I've heard is, 'Why would I want to move my business to a dying old coal town?'" (quoted in Bohman 2012).

John Dopkin, who was ninety years old in a 2012 interview, was one of only two people still living on an east side block of row homes in Shenandoah. Mr. Dopkin explained, "It's getting rough. It's getting to be a slum, believe me. So, I just have to grin and bear it." He also described his east side street in Shenandoah as the loneliest place imaginable. "I have no friends, all my friends are gone. I just lost my wife a year ago, and I'm waiting to go myself" (quoted in Bohman 2012).

The general depopulation of the region has left the place in a somber mood. While the general out-migration of the traditional white community continues, there is also an in-migration of Latinos, offsetting the population decline in a few communities. The introduction of a new and different population has created tensions around the issue of immigration and continues to make national news.

The Unhappiest Place in the United States

Since 2005, the Centers for Disease Control and Prevention (CDC) has asked individuals to report on their own life satisfaction. In the rust belt areas, about one-third of the interviewees said that they were very satisfied with their lives, compared to almost 50 percent across the United States. Self-reported unhappiness is higher in declining cites, and this tendency remains constant even when controlling for income, race, and other variables (Glaeser et al. 2014, 1). In the 2014 study of "Unhappy Cities," northeastern Pennsylvania (Scranton, Wilkes-Barre, and Hazleton) is ranked 367 out of 367 metropolitan areas (Glaeser et al. 2014, 63; Shackel 2018c).

There are many other studies that highlight the poor health and well-being of the northeastern Pennsylvania communities. For instance, in 2014, Gallup and Healthways released the report *State of American Well-Being* describing Americans' sense of well-being in terms of their emotional health, work environment, physical health, healthy behaviors, and basic access to health care. The report is meant to be a tool for employers, governments, and health care providers to help them develop strategies to improve their organizations and communities. Generally, high well-being means a healthier and more content population that is more productive and helps create economically vibrant communities. About 178,000 people across the United States were interviewed in 2013, including 1,092 residents of northeastern Pennsylvania. The survey ranked northeastern Pennsylvania 177th out of 189 metropolitan areas with regard to general well-being (Gallup-Healthways 2014). Regional newspapers, like the *Citizen's Voice* (Halpin 2014), reported: "Region's residents among most miserable." Experts in the region indicate that the results are probably related to the continuing economic downturn (Halpin 2014; Shackel 2018a, 2018b).

Using data from the CDC and credit information from Experian, a credit reporting bureau, the personal finance website BadCredit.org ranked the Scranton/Wilkes-Barre/Hazleton area fourth out of 105 metropolitan areas in the United States as being "overindulgent." The study used variables such as obesity rate, alcohol consumption, number of smokers, and average consumer debt to create an index of the most indulgent areas in the United States. The term "overindulgent" implies a lack of self-control; however, this behavior needs to be understood in the context of chronic stress. The region's respondents noted that (1) 7.8 percent of residents claim to be heavy drinkers, (2) 21.5 percent say they smoke every day, (3) there is an obesity rate of 31.95 percent, and (4) on average residents hold $28,974 in consumer debt (BadCredit.org 2015). These behaviors could be a response driven by generations of external stress (Shackel 2018c). A clinical supervisor at Wyoming Valley Alcohol and Drug Services notes that he has seen an increasing number of people seeking treatment for alcohol and drug abuse in the region. Substance abuse, he explains, follows a family cycle (quoted in Ranker 2015). Poor nutrition and high debt may be tied to transgenerational behaviors related to risk and rewards. Mental health issues like depression and substance abuse are probably indicative of the long-term impact of structural violence. However, regional mental health data is difficult to assess and is not quantified by region. On the other hand, the Commonwealth of Pennsylvania has seen a major increase of drug abuse. During 2015, drug overdoses accounted for 52,404 US deaths, including 33,091 (63.1 percent) that involved an opioid. For Pennsylvania, the drug overdose death rate increased from 2014 to 2015 by 21.5 percent and is among the highest increase in the United States (CDC 2015).

Paul Farmer (1996, 2004) has made the concept of structural violence an essential framework for researching contemporary health disparities. He examines the current social and economic structures that create health disparities and argues that it is imperative to examine the long-term history of structural violence and show how it manifests in particular settings. This approach, he notes, helps explain how these inequities developed and why they persist today. "Those who look only to powerful present-day actors to explain misery will fail to see how inequality is structured and legitimated over time. Which construction materials were used, and when, and why, and how?" (Farmer 2004, 309). Forms of structural violence and historical trauma are well documented in northeastern Pennsylvania. Poverty, malnutrition, and the degradation of the environment have created a state of poor health and well-being in the contemporary community (Shackel 2018c).

Epigenetics and the Transgenerational Impact of Structural Violence

A recent CDC study indicating death rates related to cardiovascular disease illustrates higher mortality rates in the American South, and this noninfectious disease is also prevalent throughout Appalachia, extending into the far reaches of northeastern Pennsylvania and into the southern tier of New York (Figure 3.1). Many argue that the poor health conditions found in contemporary populations are related to low education, lack of exercise, a poor diet, and poor access to medical care (De Backer 2008, Graham 2014; Watson and Preedy 2013). However, when examining variables related to cardiovascular disease (CVD), about one-half of those with CVD lack any of the conventional risk factors (Futterman and Lemberg 1998), and therefore much remains to be explained concerning the origins of this disease. I propose that the field of epigenetics may be one way of explaining the higher than average rate of CVD in northern Appalachia, which includes northeastern Pennsylvania.

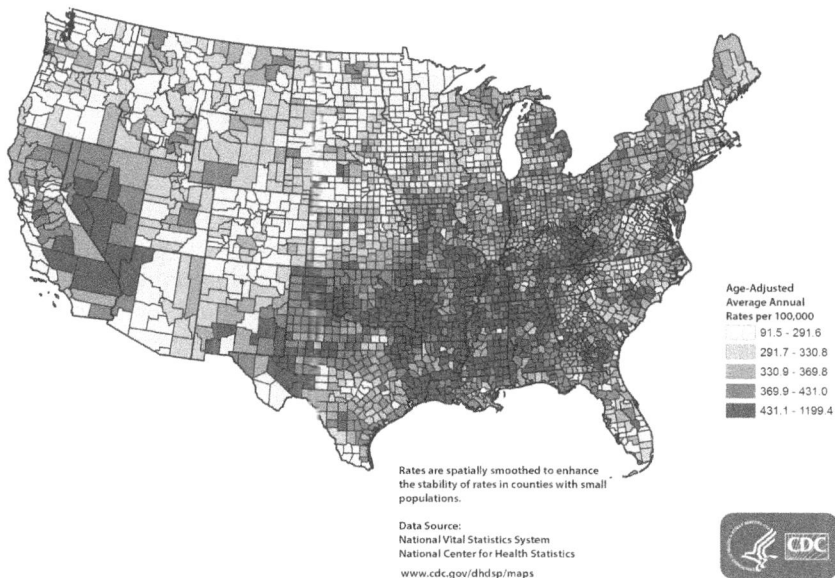

Figure 3.1. Heart disease death rate, 2014–2016, for the white population, ages 35 years and older, by county. This map was created using the Interactive Atlas of Heart Disease and Stroke, a website developed by the Centers for Disease Control and Prevention, Division for Heart Disease and Stroke Prevention, https://www.cdc.gov/dhdsp/maps/national_maps/hd_white.htm.

Epigenetics is the study of the change in genetic expression that does not involve the underlying DNA sequence. Epigenetic marks serve as on/off switches for genes, affecting how cells read genes, resulting in a change in phenotype without changing the genotype. The cells that make up different parts of the body—brain, heart, muscles—all have the same DNA. However, these cells take on different functions depending on how epigenetic marks turn on or off particular genes. Therefore, the study of epigenetics is about examining how the epigenetic marks may switch on or off and have a role in sustained generational changes—in this case, changes that may impact health and well-being (Shackel 2018c).

One of the first studies of transgenerational outcomes was an examination of babies born to mothers who were exposed to acute food shortages at the end of World War II, known as the Hunger Winter (1944–45). Using a sample of 1,808 firstborn children with mothers from cities in Holland who experienced famine conditions in utero, the study indicates that mothers who were exposed to famine conditions while pregnant had offspring with lower weights when compared to babies of nonexposed women (Lumey 1992). Subsequently, there has been a growing literature that shows that information that is not contained in the DNA sequence—epigenetic information—can be inherited from the parent to the offspring and succeeding generations (Heron 2010; Kuzawa and Sweet 2009; Susser et al. 2012; Thayer and Kuzawa 2011).

The Överkalix study, considered to be foundational research in exploring epigenetics, examined a group of males born in 1905. They were the grandsons of boys who, in their prepuberty years—a time when sperm cells are maturing—were exposed to different nutritional episodes. One group was exposed to a "feast season," and the other set was exposed to a "famine season." The "feast season" group died on average six years earlier than the grandsons of Överkalix boys who had been exposed to a "famine season" during the same prepuberty window. In many cases the cause of death of those in the "feast season" group was diabetes. The Överkalix grandfathers were transmitting a brief but important childhood *experience* to their grandsons, showing that some epigenetic marks may persist and be passed down for multiple generations (Pembrey et al. 2014).

Studies confirm the epigenetic transgenerational impact of nutrition and the outcome of high rates of CVD. Some evidence shows that individuals can be predisposed to CVD if the heart, vascular tree, kidneys, and pancreas are modified in the womb in response to maternal social stress and poor nutrition (Barker 2002; Barker and Thornburg 2013; Gluckman et al. 2008). One study (McEniry and Palloni 2010) examined a representative sample of Puerto Ricans between the ages of sixty and seventy-four. "This study found that after controlling for standard risk factors the probability of heart disease was 65% higher among individuals who were born during seasons in which the incidence of disease and poor nutrition were higher" (Steckel and Senney 2015, 5). Studies extending the Överkalix work indicate that children of mothers who suffer through famine during early pregnancy have a heightened risk of diabetes, obesity, and schizophrenia later in life (Bygren et al. 2014). Other studies show similar results (Daxinger and Whitelaw 2012; Pembrey et al. 2014).

According to the 2010 US federal census, northeastern Pennsylvania has one of the highest percentages of non-Hispanic whites of any US metropolitan area with a population over 500,000; 91.5 percent of the population claims their race as white alone. About 5.8 percent self-identify as Hispanic. While there is a steady out-migration from the area, since 2000 there has been a low-level in-migration of Hispanics to the area (*Metropolitan Area Situation & Outlook Report* 2016; US Census Bureau 2000). The region has one of the oldest populations in the United States (median age 40.2 years). When compared to 356 metropolitan areas, it has one of the lowest ratios of males (88.2) to females (100), a long-term result of the high mortality rate in the mining industry. The death rate outnumbers the birth rate Almost 30 percent of the population is living below the poverty level (US Census Bureau 2000; Metropolitan Area Situation & Outlook Report 2016). This community serves as a good population for which to examine the long-term impact of the transgenerational effects of poverty, exploitation, and general poor health in a deindustrializing region (Shackel 2018c).

When examining CDC data for coronary heart disease death rates and controlling for whites 35 years of age and older, the data indicate an extremely high death rate in the anthracite region and compares to some of the highest rates found in the United States (Figure 3.2). I believe that this high mortality rate related to CVD in northeastern Pennsylvania may in part be explained by the long-term structural violence that prevailed in this coal mining region. The deprivation of health care access, chronic stress related to poor nutrition and underemployment, and exposure to a toxic environment may have transgenerational effects and therefore impact the general health and well-being of the contemporary community. While there are many variables that lead to a region's relatively poor health and "unhappy" condition, the development of epigenetic studies provides a vehicle to understanding the transgenerational effects related to health and well-being and the results of long-term structural violence (Shackel 2018c).

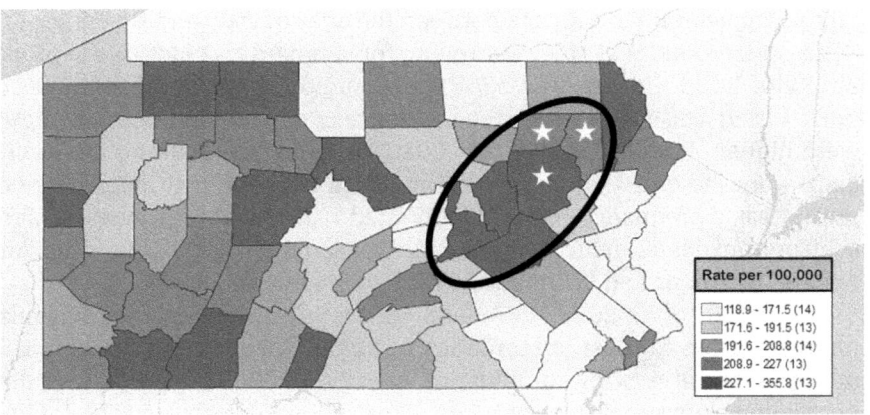

Figure 3.2. Coronary heart disease death rates for whites, 35 years and older, 2014–2016, in the anthracite coal region (encircled) of Pennsylvania. Starred counties belong to the Scranton–Wilkes-Barre–Hazleton Metropolitan Statistical Area (MSA). This map was created using the Interactive Atlas of Heart Disease and Stroke, a website developed by the Centers for Disease Control and Prevention, Division for Heart Disease and Stroke Prevention, https://nccd.cdc.gov/DHDSPAtlas/default.aspx?state=County&ol=%5b10.

Conclusion

Different forms of structural violence were rampant during the coal mining era of northeastern Pennsylvania from about the mid-nineteenth century onward (Palladino 2006). Racialized inequalities were seen as part of the natural order, or a natural outcome of history, often reinforced through religion and ideology, language and art, empirical science, and formal science (Allan 1994; Omi and Winant 1983, 51; Orser 2007, 9; Smedley 1998, 694; US Senate 1911b). The newcomers to northeastern Pennsylvania faced the stress of migration and disruption to their social networks. In northeastern Pennsylvania, the coal barons' poor treatment of their new workforce was legitimized by the racialization of the new immigrant. They were placed in jobs based on their ethnic background. As a result, the new immigrants were underemployed, earned lower wages than their peers, and lived in substandard housing. They tended to be in perpetual debt and had a limited supply and limited diversity of foodstuffs. The community faced additional stress with the loss of the coal industry, resulting in emotional trauma and continued nutritional stress.

Racial hierarchies that were naturalized in the late nineteenth century legitimized the foundation of what became a long-term history of poverty and health disparities in the area (Shackel 2018b).

About 25 percent of the anthracite region's 484 miles have been directly impacted in some way by almost two centuries of mining, and much more has been indirectly affected. The coal mining industry's collapse has led to high unemployment rates as well as a significant out-migration of its traditional population, with people abandoning the region at an alarming rate. Scattered rubble and waste are strewn throughout patches of the landscape, including black mounds of coal waste, known as culm banks, some reaching 125 feet high (Illustration 3.2). Water running through abandoned mines interacts with the coal and other surrounding materials and discharges into streams and rivers, impacting numerous waterways inside as well as outside of the region (Shackel 2017).

While commenting on the impact of mineral extraction on the global scale, Gaston Gordillo (2014, 82) points out, "Mining corporations are destroying places not just because they are obliterating rock, but because they saturated places with rubble and poison that negatively affect people and living forms. A political understanding of this spatial destruction, in other words, must be founded on an affective view of space: that is, on how destruction affects the living." Historian John Bodnar (1983, 11) writes, "No other American industry inflicted more heedless destruction on men and the environment than anthracite mining." The industry developed from the 1820s, then accelerated from the 1850s/1860s with the mechanization of coal breaking and processing. The industry immediately left an impression on many writers who described the devastating effects on the landscape and the environment (Shackel 2016).

What remains now is a scarred landscape that is dotted with mine waste, torn earth, and culm banks, all a reminder of the region's industrial past. The mined areas will remain scarred for decades, and acid mine drainage will continue as mine reclamation slowly progresses, mitigating some of these harmful impacts on the environment. Vegetation only colonizes the region very slowly, first with lichens, then wiry clumps of grass, goldenrod and briar bushes, then birch and locust trees (Marsh 1987, 347; Zawacki 2015). Culm banks dominate the landscape, and the one at Beaver Meadows, Pennsylvania (see Illustration 3.2), can be seen at a distance of over ten miles. Refuse from strip mining is visible from the ground, and aerial photographs show a moon-like surface, with craters and depressions throughout. Mining has shifted the course of waterways and polluted lakes and streams with acid runoff. Underground mining has created subsidence throughout the region, damaging highways, houses, and communities. Underground fires have also devastated communities,

Illustration 3.2. The culm bank at Beaver Meadows, Pennsylvania, is over 100 feet tall and looms over the town. Image by Paul A. Shackel.

with Centralia, Pennsylvania, where a coal seam fire that started in at least 1962 still burns today, being the most publicized incident. The region, while being depopulated and in need of a new economy, is also in search of a more effective and quicker environmental reclamation.

The historical and archaeological data from about a century ago provide some evidence that the new immigrants had low-protein and high-starch diets. If they had the opportunity to consume meat, it was often from the less preferred cuts. Contemporary cookbooks also have a plethora of recipes that tend to be high in starch. The archaeology from a 1960s context indicates that at least one family had to deal with poor health conditions and was part of the growing epidemic of diabetes and heart disease in this region, which may have been a result of the transgenerational impact of malnutrition and other stresses on this population.

These results using archaeology and other historical materials provide an interesting correlation that creates the foundation for further inquiry into understanding the long-term effects of structural violence on a community. The impact of unchecked capitalism has left this region an undesirable place to live. The higher-than-average CVD death rate among the white population probably stems in part from the legacy of the coal barons, who once controlled the everyday lives of workers and their families and exploited their large workforce. Historic forms of structural violence have left northeastern Pennsylvania without an optimistic future, as it is now known as the unhappiest place in the United States. Perhaps reconnecting people to their past and to the vibrant strengths of their ancestry and culture can help people process their past traumas and create new historical narratives that can have healing effects.

NOTE

1. University of Maryland student Toni Thomas analyzed the assemblage under the direction of Barnet Pavao Zuckerman.

CHAPTER 4

Offshoring the Textile Industry and Industrial Tragedy

Introduction

The previous chapters focused on the local and regional context of northeastern Pennsylvania, and provide an overview of some of the consequences of unchecked capitalism. The following chapters sketch the dilemma of the long-term impact of unchecked capitalism on the national and international levels. Coal extraction is practically nonexistent in the anthracite region today, and the area's textile industry, which was vibrant for more than a half a century, has also relocated out of the region to areas with cheaper, unorganized labor. The once-viable, powerful, and pro-union garment industry (International Ladies' Garment Workers' Union, or ILGWU) moved first to the American South, where labor was unorganized, and then eventually offshore to Asia. Mill owners and corporations seized the opportunity to escape organized labor and take advantage of the deep poverty found in other regions, attracting a workforce willing to labor for lower wages, often working in an unsafe environment. The exploitation that workers once faced in northeastern Pennsylvania mills has now been offshored where these conditions tend be unnoticed and unmonitored by industries, NGOs, and the Western press, unless there is a dramatic incident or catastrophe.

The Deindustrialization of Northeastern Pennsylvania

In the late nineteenth and early twentieth centuries, Paterson, New Jersey, was the industrial center of silk manufacturing. By the late nineteenth century, there was a rising demand for plain silk. The increasing mechanization of fabric production made it feasible for silk producers to utilize unskilled workers. Unlike other industries, factory location was not determined by distance to raw materials, since the raw products were coming from Japan and China. Neither were sources of fuel the driving force behind the location of the industry. Rather, it was cost and the size of the labor force that influenced factory location. The first silk mills to open outside of Paterson were in Philadelphia, and then eventually in northeastern Pennsylvania (Stepenoff 1999, 25, 27, 29). By the early twentieth century, northeastern Pennsylvania was a major economic center of the silk industry in the United States.

The late nineteenth-century construction of the world's largest silk mill occurred in Hazleton, Pennsylvania, as a result of Congress imposing a tariff on foreign silk. A Frenchman, Jean L. Duplan, expanded his silk manufacturing by constructing mills in the United States. In the early 1890s he established the Duplan Silk Company in New York. He later funded a small mill in South Bethlehem, Pennsylvania. In 1898, he was shown a site in Hazleton for the construction of a mill, which was described as a muddy, swamp-like tract scarred by mine cave-ins. An open sewer flowed through the property, and the area was surrounded by run-down shacks and urban decay. Duplan was also alerted to the recent events related to the Lattimer massacre and the potential for labor organizing in the area. However, the community rallied in support of the mill; churches throughout the city collected 25 cents from members, and banks sold bonds in order to help defray the cost of purchasing the land for the mill. A booklet published by Duplan in 1918, commemorating the twentieth anniversary of the silk mill's manufacturing in Hazleton, put a different spin on the situation. Duplan said that he came across schoolchildren that were being dismissed from school. The children were curious and friendly and he "considered this a better proof of the population than all the official records" (quoted in Tarone 2004, 44).

Duplan constructed a six hundred thousand square foot mill in Hazleton—at the time it was the world's largest silk mill. The mill went into operation in 1899 and was expanded in 1908 and again in 1909. The Duplan factory was one of the largest silk fabric enterprises in the United States, employing nearly eighteen hundred workers. By the mid-1920s, Hazleton employed three thousand people in textile mills and another two thousand in shirt factories (Sterba 1996, 9; Westmont 2019:146–150).

Bonnie Stepenoff's (1999, 30–32) research shows that even though Pennsylvania silk workers performed the same tasks as their counterparts in Paterson, they were paid 25 to 40 percent less. The percentage of female workers was much greater in Pennsylvania than in Paterson. Following the silk strike of 1900/1, some of the mill owners testified to the Industrial Commission that their industry relocated to Pennsylvania because of the availability of child labor (Stepenoff 1999, 53). Few male heads of households found work in silk mills (Stepenoff 1999, 120).

After the 1902 anthracite coal strike, silk workers testified in court as the federal government explored the working conditions in the region's industries. At the hearings in Scranton, Pennsylvania, the attorney for the miners, Clarence Darrow, called girls to testify about their working conditions and pay. Most girls testified that they worked ten-hour days and sixty hours a week. Girls as young as twelve years old testified that they worked the night shift. Some brought in the majority of their family's income. Darrow used their testimony not necessarily to discourage child labor, but rather to point out that miners did not receive adequate compensation for their work and therefore children had to be sent out to work to make ends meet for the family (Stepenoff 1999, 13). Clarence Darrow (quoted in Stepenoff 1999, 21) exclaimed:

> Is there any man so blind that he does not know why that anthracite region is dotted with silk mills? Why are they not on the parries of the West? Why are they not somewhere else? Why is it that men who make money that is spun from the lives of these little babes, men who use these children to deck their daughters and their wives—why is it that they went to Scranton and to all those towns? They went there because the miners were there. They went there just as naturally as a wild beast goes to find its prey. They went there as the hunter goes where he can find game.

The Industrial Workers of the World (IWW) worked to organize the mill workers in northeastern Pennsylvania in preparation for the Paterson Silk Strike of 1913. The textile strike of 1913 began in Hazleton on 6 February and lasted until the middle of the summer. The weavers from Duplan's Jacquard Department walked off the job, demanding that the common practice of fines for errors in garment manufacturing be discontinued. On 7 February, the strikers heard speeches from organizers from the United Textile Workers of America (UTWA) as well as from the IWW. Many of the strikers remembered that the UTWA had not helped the workers' cause during the past three strikes, so many of the mill workers quickly aligned themselves with the IWW. A list of ten demands from the workers included an increase of wages for those of various ranks, better and more sanitary working conditions, and the abolition of fines. On 13 February, the Duplan strikers voted to affiliate with the IWW (Tarone 2004, 51–53).

Miners supported the strike and prevented female household members from crossing the strike line. At times the strike became violent, with members of the IWW blocking strikers from entering the factory. After a month of violence, a type of martial law was declared by the mayor of Hazleton. By March, workers began their defection from the IWW and joined or rejoined the UTWA of the American Federation of Labor (AFL).

On 2 April, the Duplan workers ended the strike with a wage increase of between 10 and 30 percent and the work week cut from sixty hours to fifty-five hours (Tarone 2004, 60).

The Paterson Silk Strike ended in the summer of 1913, when the workers, weak and hungry, could not hold out any longer. The key reason that the capitalists defeated labor was because many of the manufacturers were able to send their orders to the Pennsylvania mills to be completed while the Paterson mills were idle. Stepenoff (1999, 83) explains that "by taking jobs in the mills and bringing home their wages these young men and women expressed great loyalty to their parents and siblings. It would have been difficult for them to put aside this loyalty and join the IWW in the face of parental opposition."

The Duplan operations expanded quickly, and by 1918 the factory had three wings with 558,550 square feet built on 23.8 acres. Included in the expansion were several amenities not found elsewhere in Hazleton. The Duplan complex had two lunchrooms, one for men and one for women. It also had a first aid station, a place for school classes, and separate athletic facilities for men and women. The facility had baseball and football fields, pool tables, and a swimming pool (Tarone 2004, 44).

The silk industry in northeastern Pennsylvania peaked in the 1920s and began its gradual decline in the 1930s (Stepenoff 1999, 13). The textile workers in Hazleton joined the call from the UTWA for a general strike on 1 September 1934. In total about four hundred thousand textile workers from across the country walked off their jobs. It was the largest strike in a single industry in US history. On 12 September 1934, unionists called for a city-wide general strike in support of the striking mill workers, and the city was "still for a day" (Sterba 1996, 4). Many of the mill towns affected by the strike fell on hard times very quickly because the mill was the only form of employment in these communities (Sterba 1996, 5).

The 1930s and 1940s saw the acceleration of runaway garment factories in northeastern Pennsylvania (Wolensky 2003, 91–92). It was easy to load machinery on trucks and transport it to new factories. The remaining mills in the anthracite region were transformed and began producing other fabrics, like rayon, with new, updated machinery (Stepenoff 1999, 13). During the Great Depression, the Pennsylvania Bureau of Women and Children in the State Department of Labor and Industry did a survey of runaway factories in Allentown, Doylestown, and Shamokin and discovered that "pittance wages predominated" (quoted in Wolensky 2003, 93). The UTWA's Cotton Garment and Miscellaneous Trade Department reported:

> No other state in the land offers such shocking contrasts as does Pennsylvania. Her beauty and squalor actually lie side by side. Here are filthy mining towns with their warped houses and crooked alley streets where poverty is the byword and death the great emancipator;

where thousands are slaving in misery while the abundant gift of nature, denied to those who toil, are generally heaped upon the countryside. (Gingold, quoted in Wolensky 2003, 96)

The exploitative conditions of the textile workers became clear in the region:

> In recent years the chiseling, runaway garment manufacturer has also come to prey upon the poverty-stricken industrial workers in this setting. Pennsylvania is fertile territory for the garment chiseler who is forever seeking a cheap labor market and to exploit the helpless. One cannot but feel the stirring of the masses, the slow grumbling of the downtrodden whose sisters and wives have become the garment workers in the Kingdom of Coal. (Gingold, quoted in Wolensky 2003, 96)

Francis Perkins, Labor Secretary to President Franklin Roosevelt, also wrote about the runaway industries:

> His workforce is made up of the daughters and wives of local wage earners who have been out of work for months or even years and whose family situation is desperate. The boss sets the wage rates, figures the pay slips, and determines the hours of work. His reply to complaints is, "Quit if you do not like it." In the runaway shop conditions are usually far below standard and picture of such a plant is a look back to the sweatshops at the turn of the century. (Perkins, quoted in Wolensky 2003, 92)

The Duplan silk mill closed in 1953, and other textile mills in the region began to move to the American South, although some textile factories survived in the region through the 1980s. When these industries closed, new ones did not develop and replace them. There was nowhere for people to go for employment, as it coincided with the downturn of the coal industry. Economic hard times were felt throughout the region, and a slow outmigration began. The closing of industry had a ripple effect in Hazleton and the rest of the region, and stores began to close along the main streets. By 1956, Hazleton had an unemployment rate of 25 percent. Its population, which reached thirty-eight thousand during the World War II era, has declined to about twenty-five thousand residents (Tarone 2004, 128).

A healthy economy requires perpetual reincarnation, and northeastern Pennsylvania did not attract a major industry after the decline in coal and the exit of the textile industry (Wolensky 2003). Barry Bluestone and Bennett Harrison (1982, 12) write,

> With industry moving so rapidly, those who lose their jobs in the older sectors of the economy rarely have a chance at employment in the new ones—even within the same region. As a result, the creative de-

structive process has become synonymous with our conception of the "throwaway" culture. Instead of recycling people and communities through the development process, the pace of capital mobility has become so fast that people and communities are carelessly discarded to make room for new ones.

In the case of northeastern Pennsylvania, the runaway garment factories initially moved to the American South, and then offshore to American territories in the Pacific, and then eventually to South Asian developing countries. Little has replaced the garment industry or the coal industry in northeastern Pennsylvania, and the economy still struggles to recover. As L. A. Tarone (2004) notes, "Hazleton has been 'looking toward the future' for virtually all of the past five decades."

Commonwealth of Northern Mariana Islands

Manufacturers continue to look for new ways to decrease costs in order to maintain or increase market demand. At times new technologies are the answer, and other times manufacturers find a less expensive labor force. Part of the garment industry's movement to offshore production was the migration to US territories in the western Pacific, like the Commonwealth of the Northern Mariana Islands (CNMI). This territory is located in Micronesia and consists of fifteen islands in the western Pacific Ocean, about 3,900 miles west of Hawaii. As a result of World War II, the United Nations combined the Micronesian Islands along with the Mariana Islands to form the Trust Territory of the Pacific Islands (TTPI). The United States agreed to be the trustee. In the late 1960s, TTPI islands discussed the nature of their relationship with the United States. While many of the islands wanted more independence, the Mariana Islands decided on a closer relationship with the United States. The Northern Mariana Islands voted to become a US commonwealth in 1975, and Congress approved this status in 1976 (Cruz Cuison 2000, 67). Inhabitants of the Northern Mariana Islands became US citizens, though governed by their own constitution. They were exempt from several US federal laws, such as minimum wage law, in order to promote economic growth and attract businesses. The commonwealth is allowed to set its own immigration policy (Story 5a n.d.). Until recently, the US Immigration and Nationality Act and the federal minimum wage provision of the Fair Labor and Standards Act did not apply to the CNMI. This exemption was part of the agreement that created the relationship between the Marianas and the United States that became official in 1986, with an agreement known as the Covenant to Establish the Commonwealth of the Northern Mariana

Islands in Political Union with the United States. These exemptions led to significant economic development, as well as a dramatic influx of workers who were exploited, cheated, and indentured. The garment industry, nonexistent on the island in the early 1980s, quickly developed as the island's major industry (Cruz Cuison 2000, 63–64, 71; Little and Shackel 2014).

Federal law allowed manufacturers from CNMI to export clothing to the American mainland duty-free and largely without quotas. While there was a significant campaign by the ILGWU to "look for the union label" in clothing, garments made in the CNMI used "Made in America" labels. The garment workers produced clothing for some of the top American shopping brands, such as Arrow, Liz Claiborne, Gap, Montgomery Ward, Geoffrey Beene, Eddie Bauer, and Levi's (Shenon 1993). In the 1980s and 1990s, American labor unions argued that the low wages paid to garment workers in the Northern Marianas was stealing jobs from textile workers in the United States. "We have rules for protecting products, such as copyright laws, but seemingly we have no rules to protect the workers who produce the product—if they happen to be in Saipan," said Arthur Gundersheim, director of international affairs for the Amalgamated Clothing and Textile Workers Union (quoted in Shenon 1993).

Loopholes and poor enforcement of US immigration and wage laws encouraged Asian-based garment manufacturers to flock to the island along with tens of thousands of indentured workers. Within a decade, twenty factories were established, most owned by foreign investors. Every year, thousands of foreign workers from China, the Philippines, and other countries in Asia were flown to Saipan, lured by the prospect of good American jobs. In 1993, the Northern Marianas had about 42,000 people, of which Saipan was the largest population center. However, more than half (23,000) were foreign workers. By 1999 there were 27,000 US citizens and 40,000 foreign workers on the island (Bales 2004, 2005, 96–97; Little and Shackel 2014; Shenon 1993; Story 1 n.d.).

Federal labor laws applied to the commonwealth except, until recently, minimum wage labor law. However, enforcing these labor laws was difficult, since the main regional office of the Labor Department is thousands of miles away. Furthermore, the owner of several garment factories also owned the largest newspaper. In addition, the Catholic Church closed its human rights advocate position in the commonwealth (Bales 2005, 96–97; Shenon 1993; Story 6 n.d.). The Commonwealth of the Northern Mariana Islands admitted immigrants as temporary workers, and the law limited work contracts to one year. The textile workers labored seventy to eighty hours per week without overtime pay. CNMI labor laws allowed textile manufacturers to pay below minimum wages. In 1993, garment workers made $2.15 an hour, about half of the US minimum wage. One garment worker said, "We come here because we make more money here than in China, and because the recruiters in China tell us that Saipan is part of America" (quoted in Shenon 1993). From 1997 to 2007, garment workers earned $3.05 an hour compared with US minimum wage of $5.15 an hour in 1997 and $5.85 an hour in 2007 (Vallejera 2007).

One garment factory worker reported that she was forced to work overtime without compensation in order for the factory to meet production quotas. The supervisor yelled constantly and beat the workers "whenever he felt like it" (quoted in Collier 1999). "A lot of the females were told you work during the day in the garment factory and then at night you can go and work in a club and they'd force them into prostitution at night. . . . If some female got pregnant, they either had to go back to China to give birth or have a forced abortion" (Wendy Doromol, quoted in Ydstie 2006). There were an estimated ten thousand foreign workers who overstayed their work permits, marooned after being cheated by labor contractors (Collier 1999).

Foreign workers paid an exorbitant recruitment fee that took several years to pay off. They signed contracts that waived several basic human rights such as joining a union, striking, attending religious services, marrying, or resigning. Having a large debt to repay placed pressure on the worker to be silent about the abusive working conditions. Non-English speakers were seen as a benefit to the textile industry, since they were less apt to file a complaint. Workers could not gain US citizenship or be protected by US civil and social rights. "Only a few countries and no democratic society have immigrant policies similar to the CNMI. The closest equivalent is Kuwait" (Story 2b n.d.).

As an example of the illegal recruiting practices, in 1997 workers from Bangladesh, where the annual per capita income was about $250, paid $5,000 to come to Saipan and work. They were told by labor contractors that they were going to Saipan, USA, the land of the free—located only a train ride away from Los Angeles. When they got to Saipan, there was no job (Collier 1999). While the recruiters were fined $104,684 and ordered to pay the Bangladeshis, the government was unable to collect (Collier 1999). One Bangladeshi stated, "Now I know that the American flag doesn't mean much." He added, "In World War II, thousands of American soldiers died to put the flag in these islands. But I ask, what for? Where is justice? It's now the responsibility of the Americans to restore the dignity of that flag" (Collier 1999).

The workers faced substandard living conditions. Manufacturers placed them in oversized plywood shacks with tin roofs that served as workers' barracks. Often, they had no regular water or electricity. One dwelling had a room that slept eight, which also served as a kitchen. While federal regulations required that workers receive a minimum of 100 square feet of space per person to cook and sleep, in one instance there were six workers in one room of 190 square feet (Shenon 1993). One worker said that they were afraid to complain because they feared that their bosses would send them back to China and take away all of their owed money. Their families, workers said, needed the money. The workers complained of living in virtual captivity. Their houses were surrounded by barbed wire, which was patrolled by guards (Shenon 1993). Wendy Doromol, a human rights worker, explained in 2006, "The barbed wire around the factories face inward so that the mostly women couldn't get out" (Wendy Doromol, quoted in Ydstie 2006). One company had a dormitory with 120 workers with three working toilets and five showers. "They didn't respect us, and they made me feel like I wasn't a human being," one woman said (quoted in Collier 1999).

As many of these abuses were exposed in the mid-1990s, the garment manufacturers were sanctioned by the US Labor Department. The Northern Marianas' reputation of dismal working conditions led Democratic lawmakers and the Clinton administration to attempt to eliminate the islands' longtime exemption from federal immigration, customs, and minimum wage laws. As a result, the island's government hired lobbyist Jack Abramoff and paid millions for his work (Ydstie 2006). Abramoff flew more than a hundred congressional aides and members of Congress to the island on fact-finding trips. They were usually shown a clean, well-run factory, and then beach time and golf (Ydstie 2006). In 1998, while the Interior Department investigated the abuses of guest workers, Abramoff stated: "Most of the workers on the island would be violently upset if they understood what these self-proclaimed helpers of the workers are up to, which is in essence destroying their jobs and destroying their families' opportunities" (quoted in Ydstie 2006).

The Republican leadership blocked these attempts to eliminate exemptions for a long time (Collier 1999). In 1997, Rep. Tom DeLay (R-TX), the House majority whip at the time, visited the island on New Year's Eve. As a guest of the CNMI government, he stated that he would fight any federal takeover of Saipan's immigration and labor laws. ABC News recorded DeLay telling his host, "You are a shining light for what is happening in the Republican Party, and you represent everything that is good about what we are trying to do in America and leading the world in the free-market system" (Shields 1998, A7; Ydstie 2006). Global Survival Network, a human rights group, recorded Delay reassuring Willie Tan, the owner of the island's biggest garment firm, that his business would be protected. As a member of the House Republican leadership, he controlled the schedule and would ensure that reform legislation didn't get a hearing (Ydstie 2006).

Abramoff enlisted the help of Ralph Reed, head of the Faith and Freedom Coalition, a large organization with lobbyists in fifty state capitals and an annual budget of $100 million. Reed's direct mail company, Millennium Marketing, conducted a mailing campaign and urged Alabama Christians to write their local congressman to oppose the labor and immigration reforms in the CNMI. Reed explained that the reforms were a scheme orchestrated by the Left and organized labor. The reforms would keep workers from being "exposed to the teachings of Jesus Christ." His company explained it was just trying to encourage "grassroots citizens to promote the propagation of the Gospel" and that many of the workers were "converted to the Christian faith and return to China with Bibles in hand" (quoted in Moyers and Winship 2012).

In 1998, Rep. George Miller (D-CA) visited the Saipan factories in the CNMI, and later introduced legislation to raise the island minimum wage and impose federal control of immigration. The *Seattle Post-Intelligencer* (Shields 1998, A7) reported that Miller had little success in the House minority. It took almost a decade for this legislation to pass, in the fall of 2007 (Little and Shackel 2014).

The US Department of Labor had to intercede in 1998 after five island employers refused to pay more than $2.1 million in overtime pay owed to 1,315 workers. In 1999, the US labor secretary, Alexis Herman, said, "We must stop the exploitation of workers on these islands. We will continue to hold employers accountable and will work to get U.S. minimum wage standards . . . extended to the Northern Marianas" (quoted in Collier 1999). Another government official stated, "What's more important is that none of these abuses are permitted under U.S. law, and the Northern Marianas shouldn't be able to pick and choose between the laws of the land just to benefit a few people" (quoted in Collier 1999).

In 2007, local control of the minimum wage was superseded by the United States Congress. For over a decade the minimum wage in the CNMI was $3.05 an hour. (To put this in perspective, consider that the minimum wage in the US in 1980 was $3.10). After 2007, the local minimum wage in the CNMI was to be increased by $0.50 per hour annually in order to catch up with the US standard (Vallejera 2007). In May 2008, Congress passed a law mandating that US immigration laws apply to the Commonwealth of the Northern Mariana Islands, and they superseded and replaced all local immigration laws. Transition to US immigration laws began on 28 November 2009 (Misulich 2011). All of these changes and government regulations placed the commonwealth garment industry under severe economic pressure, and eventually all of the garment factories closed by 2009 (de la Torre 2007). The garment industry in the CNMI has migrated to other low-wage regions of the world, while labor abuses continue on these islands involving two other booming industries, gambling and entertainment, including the sex trade (Ydstie 2006). Labor issues related to the Mariana Islands still exist. For instance, one item on the 2012 GOP platform stated, "No minimum wage for the Mariana Islands. The Pacific territories should have flexibility to determine the minimum wage, which has seriously restricted progress in the private sector" (Moyers and Winship 2012). Despite lawmakers' attempts to deregulate the labor laws in the CNMI, many of the manufacturers have migrated to other developing countries in South Asia (Little and Shackel 2014).

Bangladesh

When the garment industry left the CNMI, many of the factories migrated to countries in Asia, joining other recently established garment companies. In places like Bangladesh, garment manufacturing has led to impressive growth in Bangladesh's overall GDP (Chakravartty and Luce 2013). Recently, Bangladesh has become the second-largest garment producer in the world, with a trillion-dollar industry.

The textile industry has been a major part of the South Asian economy for many decades. When Bangladesh gained its independence from Pakistan in 1972, the large textile mills were nationalized. The privatization of the industry began in the 1980s, and was accelerated after 1986, as a result of the government signing the International Monetary Fund's structural adjustment policies. Despite agreeing to the pursuit of "free markets," the Bangladesh government played a significant role in regulating the industry and fighting against workers' attempts to unionize (Chakravartty and Luce 2013).

Since 1986, there has been an explosion in the growth of the ready-made garment (RMG) industry worldwide. The industry now accounts for close to 80 percent of Bangladesh's overall exports (Chakravartty and Luce 2013). By 2010, Bangladesh had about five thousand garment factories, second only to China and more than twice the number in Indonesia and Vietnam. "They are undercutting each other over two to three billion dollars of new business each year," said Kasra Ferdows, a professor of operations management at Georgetown University. "It creates a dog-eat-dog business where there are a lot people on the margins who will cut corners" (quoted in Srivastava 2013).

Bangladesh's exports tripled between 2005 and 2010, partially as a result of the collapse of the CNMI textile industry, and are expected to triple again by 2020 to almost $50 billion a year. The major increase in production is because of the relatively lower wages the industry pays its workers compared to other RMG industry regions. In 2009, workers in Dhaka were paid $47 per month compared to $235 in Shenzhen and $100 in Hanoi, according to the Japan External Trade Organization. While being paid very low wages, the workers also toil under extreme conditions (Srivastava 2013).

Bangladesh has 3.6 million garment workers, most of whom are women (about 12 percent of all women in Bangladesh), and the majority are between the ages of fifteen and thirty. The garment factories favor women because they are seen as better at sewing—and more compliant. Sheikh Hasina, the country's female prime minister, sees the large number of women workers as a symbol of empowerment. However, Human Rights Watch noted that there is an urgent need for better worker protections for Bangladesh's workforce (*Al Jazeera* 2013b; Srivastava 2013).

Most of the garment industry is located in export processing zones where companies are exempt from many basic laws—and pay little in taxes. The large retailers and the garment factory owners reap the profits, while the number of working poor grows. Because the garment industry is a very large proportion of Bangladesh's GDP, the government does little to disrupt this system of profit making—at home and abroad (Chakravartty and Luce 2013).

According to the British nonprofit War on Want, about 70 percent of the 988 garment workers surveyed in Bangladesh claimed that they were verbally abused by their bosses, and over 40 percent had been beaten. One-third said that they had been sexually harassed, and more than half of the women interviewed were not allowed to take their legally guaranteed maternity leave of one hundred days. The majority worked until the last weeks of pregnancy and were often fired when they left to give birth (Srivastava 2013).

Unsafe Conditions in the Garment Industry in Bangladesh

The Collapse of the Rana Plaza

The RMG industry has created large profit margins for Western retailers while its workers labor in unsafe conditions (Srivastava 2013). Manufacturers are known to cut corners, usually at the expense of safe work conditions, in order to maintain profits. The New York Triangle Shirtwaist Factory fire of 1911 killed 146 workers, and while workplace safety regulations were enacted after that catastrophic event, many tragic incidents continue well into the twenty-first century and remain prevalent in the new manufacturing centers in developing countries. Bangladesh has a history of workplace disasters because of poor safety conditions. For instance, 64 people were killed when a factory collapsed in 2005 in a suburb of Savar (the site of the Rana Plaza). In 2006, at least 22 people were killed when another building collapsed in Dhaka. In November 2012, a factory fire killed 112 garment workers at the Tazreen Fashion Factory near Dhaka. More recently, a fire in 2012 killed about 260 people in Pakistan (*Al Jazeera* 2013a, 2013b; Alam 2013; Alam and Hossain 2013; Butler 2013; Hossain 2013).

The garment industry disaster that gained notable international attention occurred in 2013 at the Rana Plaza, located about fifteen miles outside of Dhaka, Bangladesh. The eight-story building housed a variety of businesses, including a bank and five factories employing 3,122 garment workers. On 23 April 2013, workers noticed a large crack in the building. The police ordered that the building be evacuated, and the bank on the second floor told its workers not to come in the next day (*Al Jazeera* 2013a; Alam and Blake 2013; Chakravartty and Luce 2013). Abdur Razzak Khan, an engineer, inspected the building; he appeared on television the night before the collapse and said he had told Sohel Rana, the owner of the Rana Plaza, that the building should be evacuated. The police also issued an evacuation order; however, Rana told workers that the building was safe, and garment factory managers told them to report to their jobs (Hossain 2013).

The following day, 24 April 2013, the garment factories ignored the warnings and opened their facilities. The owners and managers of the textile factories demanded their employees come to work and threatened them with heavy penalties if they did not. It was when the morning shift started, and the large generators were turned on, that the building collapsed, raining down concrete beams. Some people died instantly. Others lost hands or legs to amputation during their rescue or afterward. Hundreds of others were trapped alive in triple-digit temperatures (Yardley 2013b). The Rana Plaza collapse is the deadliest disaster to affect the garment industry (Alam and Blake 2013). The collapse killed 1,129 people and injured 2,500 more. The victims were mostly young Muslim women, and is an example of globally networked violence. The Rana Plaza incident adds to the mounting number of deaths in the South Asian garment industry (*Al Jazeera* 2013a; Alam 2013; Chakravartty and Luce 2013).

The architect of the building explained that the structure was not designed to handle heavy industrial equipment; rather, it was designed in 2004 as a shopping mall. The top three floors were illegally added at a later date (Hossain 2013). "We designed the building to have three stories for shops and another two for offices. I don't know how the additional floors were added and how factories were allowed on the top floors," the architect explained. "Don't ask me anything else. This is now a sensitive issue," he said before hanging up the phone (quoted in Hossain 2013).

The news media eventually revealed that the building's construction was illegal. The owner, Sohel Rana, a local politician, obtained permits from the mayor instead of local building authorities. The glass-fronted factory complex was constructed on a swamp (Srivastava 2013). Rana used substandard construction materials for the building, which was completed in 2006. Government officials reported that substandard building materials, along with the vibration of the heavy machines used by the factories, led to the collapse (Hossain 2013).

Workers Protest in the Midst of the Ruins in Dhaka over Factory Deaths

Countless spaces are obliterated every day, either through the destruction of landscapes to build, the destruction of landscapes for extraction, or the destruction of landscapes because of tragic episodes as a result of unchecked capitalism. Gavan Lucas (2013, 193) reminds us that ruins provide a sense of mortality. While a ruin can act as a sign of the end of a society or culture, they can also become reminders of a past civilization or a way of life. Once they are transformed into something deemed historic, or a monument to past heritage, they can become a reflection on history and help reinforce a narrative of progress (Lucas 2013, 192). Georg Simmel ([1911] 1959), writing about ruins, described the tension between nature and the forces of decay and the human spirit that had transformed natural raw material, and recognized that nature is transforming human labor into something new again (Lucas 2013, 193). Lucas (2013, 194) also notes that:

> At a superficial level, modern ruins (think of a derelict factory) can indeed be seen to stand almost diametrically opposed to the classical ruin (think of an abandoned medieval abbey), incorporating a series of connected dichotomies with respective positive and negative valuations. Where classical ruins evoke an aesthetic of attraction, the modern ruin is simply garbage. Indeed, while the classical ruin seems to exhibit graceful decay through natural processes, the modern ruin is like a fresh carcass spilling out its guts, where intentional human abandonment or destruction is often as prevalent as nature reclaiming its own.

After the Rana Plaza incident, thousands from the community protested in the streets in the shadow of the ruins for better working conditions, and they called for Rana to be hanged (*Al Jazeera* 2013a). Protesting near the ruins was a way to reinforce the sense of mortality and the fragility of life for the garment workers. Sohel Rana, owner of the building, tried to flee the country, but was detained near the Indian border and flown back to the capital. Prime Minister Sheikh Hasina ordered the arrest of Rana and the owners of the garment factories housed in the structure (Calamur 2013). When Rana was captured, the event was announced by loudspeaker at the disaster site, drawing cheers and applause from rescue workers and the people waiting to find out the fate of their family members (Alam and Blake 2013). "The human-faced beast who had built a death trap here was arrested while trying to flee the country," said a local government minister while touring the ruins (*Al Jazeera* 2013a).

The four government engineers who approved the construction of buildings were also arrested (*Al Jazeera* 2013a). Rana was charged with negligence, illegal construction, and coercion of workers, crimes punishable by a maximum of seven years in prison. Khan, the engineer who inspected the building the night before the collapse, was arrested as well. Police said he had worked as a consultant when Rana illegally added the top three floors (Hossain 2013). Shamsul Haque Tuku, deputy home minister, said police arrested Bazlus Samad, managing director of New Wave Apparels Ltd., and Mahmudur Rahman Tapash, the company chairman (*Al Jazeera* 2013b). The police also arrested the managers of Tazreen Fashion for a tragedy that occurred the previous year. The managers locked workers inside the building after fire alarms went off, culminating in the deaths of 260 workers (Clark 2013).

On International Workers' Day, 1 May, thousands of protesting workers paraded through central Dhaka to demand safer working conditions as well as the death penalty for the owner of Rana Plaza. While protests developed in Savar, the district just outside Dhaka where the Rana Plaza was located, the demonstrations spread throughout Bangladesh to other cities, where protesters threw stones and set fire to vehicles (*Al Jazeera* 2013b). Violence erupted in other parts of Dhaka and in the southeastern city of Chittagong, where hundreds of garment workers took to the streets to protest. They blocked roads and vandalized vehicles. Government officials closed garment factories in Dhaka for fear of violence (*Al Jazeera* 2013b).

Protests continued throughout the year for better working conditions and better pay. On 22 September 2013, police fired rubber bullets and tear gas into a crowd of protesters in Dhaka demanding a minimum wage of 8,114 takas ($100) a month. In November, a ten-story garment factory in Gazipur, which supplied Western brands, was burned down by workers angered over rumors of a worker's death in police firing (Quadir 2013).

Who Is to Blame?

Managers forced workers back into the factories on 24 April 2013, because they were under pressure to complete orders for buyers in a timely fashion. The quick turnaround is a product of rapid changes in design, also known as fast fashion. While collectively organized trade unions could have responded to the pressure of management, unions have been discouraged by the government because it would increase workforce costs, thereby threatening the slim profits made in the Bangladesh garment industry (Burk 2014; Wolff 2013).

Among the garment makers in the Rana Plaza included Phantom Apparels, Phantom Tac, Ether Tex, New Wave Style, and New Wave Bottoms. The New Wave companies make clothing for several major North American and European retailers (Alam and Blake 2013). A growing number of US companies—including Walmart, Sears, Disney, and Dickies—have been linked to the Rana Plaza building collapse. For instance, Walmart's Faded Glory brand shorts were found among the ruins of the building. Walmart and Sears have tried to distance themselves from the the incident. Walmart stated that they had cut ties with the factory months earlier; however, a subcontractor sent work to the factory. After the Rana Plaza incident, Walmart announced the termination of the business relationship with that subcontractor. While Sears announced that they did not source from this factory, entries in account books amid the ruins indicate the factory took orders from Sears (Clark 2013).

Many of the big retailer companies like Walmart, Gap, H&M, and hundreds of others have long ignored any request to address safety concerns for the workers in the Bangladeshi garment industry. A coalition of NGOs and workers' organizations have been demanding the development of an independent monitoring program that would address some of the basic safety regulations. Up until the Rana Plaza incident only two companies (Phillips van Heusen, which represents brands such as Calvin Klein and Tommy Hilfiger, and German-based Tchibo) had participated. Larger companies like Walmart refused to allow workers to have a voice in ensuring their safety in the workplace in Bangladesh. They deflected criticism by promising self-regulation and investing in public relations–driven charity (Chakravartty and Luce 2013).

When 112 people died in the Tazreen Fashion Factory fire in November 2012, there were widespread pledges to improve worker safety standards; however, little changed, which contributed to the tragedy at the Rana Plaza (Alam and Blake 2013). The European Union has since placed pressure on the Bangladeshi government and said that it would restrict Bangladesh's access to its market if the government failed to ensure that basic labor standards were enforced. The EU trade commissioner stated, "Not because we want to hurt Bangladesh, but because what is happening is simply not acceptable. From a humane point of view, we cannot afford that, and we have to do something about it" (quoted in Hossain 2013). In 2013, the Bangladeshi government agreed to International Labor Organization proposals that include worker protections and the right to unions (Srivastava 2013).

In 2014, a team of researchers from the New York University Stern Center for Business and Human Rights investigated working conditions and workers' safety in Bangladesh. Their report points out that only eight of 3,425 factories inspected had "remedied violations enough to pass a final inspection" despite the international community's $280 million commitment to improve Bangladesh's RMG industry (Labowitz and Baumann-Pauly 2014; White 2015).

On 14 June 2016, Sohel Rana and seventeen others were indicted for violating building codes in the construction of the Rana Plaza. In 2017, Sohel Rana received the maximum three-year sentence for failing to declare his personal wealth to Bangladesh's anti-graft commission. Rana and thirty-seven others still face murder charges related to the Rana Plaza incident and could receive the death penalty if they are found guilty of murder over the complex's collapse (*Al Jazeera* 2017).

Memorializing

The piles of destruction as a result of various forms of unchecked capitalism defy our definitions of ruins. "The paradox of modern ruins is that they are not antique and thus hold little utopian value. In fact, if contemplated for too long, they can reveal the contradictions of progress. This may be one reason why projects of demolition often proceed rapidly in urban settings, even if all that replaces failed projects are wastelands and vacant lots" (Dawdy 2010, 769). Expanding on the work by Andreas Huyssen (2010), Gavin Lucas explains that ruins challenge the belief of unending progress. They represent the fear of future apocalypse and show that modern may no longer be modern. "The recent ruin haunts modernity in a way no ancient ruin can" (Lucas 2013, 196).

In the midst of the destruction as a result of unchecked capitalism at Rana Plaza, on 1 May 2013 (International Workers' Day), Pope Francis spoke out against the working conditions in the Bangladesh factories:

> A headline that really struck me on the day of the tragedy in Bangladesh was "Living on 38 euros a month." That is what the people who died were being paid. This is called slave labour. Today in the world this slavery is being committed against something beautiful that God

has given us—the capacity to create, to work, to have dignity. How many brothers and sisters find themselves in this situation! Not paying fairly, not giving a job because you are only looking at balance sheets, only looking at how to make a profit. That goes against God! (Quoted in Pullella 2013)

On 30 August 2013, community members and survivors of the Rana Plaza tragedy, along with workers' rights activists, inaugurated a memorial at the site of the tragedy. It has two fists thrusting toward the sky grasping a hammer and sickle. It is symbolic of the many people who were struggling for their lives, struggling to climb out of the ruins. The hammer and sickle are a commentary on capitalism. When the police tried to halt the erection of the memorial, they were unable to stop the masses of people involved in the ceremony. It remains the only memorial for the tragedy (Yardley 2013a). Afterward, workers continued to protest the conditions surrounding their labor, including on the first anniversary of the collapse (Illustration 4.1).

Illustration 4.1. Thousands of garment workers and their unions rally on the first anniversary of the Rana Plaza collapse. Bangladesh Federation of Workers Solidarity (BFWS), Solidarity Center, https://www.flickr.com/photos/62762640@N02/16237258782/in/photostream/.

Unassuming Revolutionaries

Challenges to social and economic conditions can come from many different and sometimes unexpected places. What follows is an amazing and mostly unknown story about how the actions of one unassuming woman led to a revolution and changed a country, and perhaps a good portion of the Arab world. News media throughout the world reported that new technologies, like Twitter and Facebook, helped to coordinate the spring uprisings in Egypt that led to the downfall of Hosni Mubarak in 2011. However, very few people realize that the revolution began five years earlier in Egypt's industrial heartland in the small mill town of Mahalla, which lies in the Nile Delta, known for its cotton industry. In December 2006, a middle-aged mill worker, Wedad Demerdash, was spurred into action. Despite long working hours, she could not afford to buy meat for her family. Eating chicken was a rare event, only about once a month. Wedad led her female coworkers on strike, marching on the factory grounds and chanting, "Where are the men? Here are the women." This action shamed the men into joining the protest, and after three days the workers won the strike (Shackel 2013; Sly 2011, A9).

Mahalla has become known for its workers' militancy, and the events in the city set the tone for the rest of the nation. If the workers at Mahalla go on strike and win, the rest of the country will follow. The success at Mahalla in 2006 stimulated a strike wave throughout 2007. The Mahalla workers took the lead in calling for a subsequent national strike on 6 April 2008, calling for a national minimum wage. Those who follow the Egyptian labor movement claim that it was the success of the strikes at Mahalla and the militancy of the labor force demanding subsistence wages that led to the subsequent revolution in 2011. Indeed, the "6th of April" Facebook group, named after the national strike, became a major vehicle to rally the protesters of Cairo's Tahrir Square in January 2011. These labor strikes continue, and the new government in Egypt will need to recognize the increasingly organized labor movement if the country's unrest is to subside (Shackel 2013; Sly 2011, A9).

Mentioning the heroics of a few people who changed a community and a nation is a simple lesson—that we too can make a difference in the way communities see themselves in the past and the present. This public memory has larger implications tied to issues of social and political justice as control of narrative plays out in communities and societies. When doing our heritage work, the challenge is to redefine the way people think about class, conflict, human rights, and representation. It is about addressing issues of political and social justice and making these issues part of the narrative structure.

CHAPTER 5

Offshoring Mining Industries and Tragedy

Illusion of Capitalism

In the nineteenth century, the British had developed some of the best engineering practices for mining. However, in the interest of saving time and money, many colliery operations in the anthracite region ignored these practices because the cautionary efforts would eat into the coal operators' profits. Many of these mines in the anthracite region were prone to poor ventilation, inadequate timbered mines, explosions, roof falls, fires, and floods. Many hundreds of miners were crippled or killed each year because coal barons ignored many of these advances in safety. The high frequency of disasters was a trade problem. Coal operators ignored geologists' reports and continued to use cheap technology at the cost of many human lives. Anthony Wallace noted that the coal operators bemused themselves with illusions. In the mid-nineteenth century, "They told themselves and the world that the absence of high enough tariff on British iron was keeping coal prices too low to make a profit, and that careless miners and Irish revolutionaries were largely responsible for the high rate of disasters. These illusions helped the owners and operators . . . to keep on producing coal to fuel the Industrial Revolution" (Wallace 1987, 6).

Whenever there was an accident that found its way into the court system, the English and American courts often ruled in favor of the industrialists. The "fellow servant" rule asserted that an injured employee could not hold an employer responsible if a fellow employee caused the accident. It also asserted that the employer was free to leave his master's employment if he considered the conditions to be unsafe. If a worker continued his employment with a negligent "fellow servant," the worker assumed the risk of the job. The rule would eventually include the risk imposed by an employer who did not provide a reasonably safe workplace. Because of the precedents of early court cases, issues such as contributory negligence, the "fellow servant" rule, and assumption of risk virtually nullified the employer's risk and responsibility for his workers (Wallace 1987, 279–80; Shackel 2018).

Only after a series of mining disasters and persistent protests by workers for decent pay and increased safety regulations did the government act to protect workers. Some of these protests were the results of accidents, which in some cases had led to fatalities. While mining continues to be a dangerous occupation, most of the mines currently operating in northeastern Pennsylvania are nonunion, and many of the workers view unionizing as an unnecessary expense. They believe that the federal regulations are enough to protect them. Such regulations include the Coal Mine Safety Act of 1969, which developed as a response to the explosion at Farmington Number 9 in West Virginia, in which seventy-eight miners were killed. The Mine Safety and Health Administration (MSHA) was established to enforce the laws. In the early twentieth century, coal mining fatalities averaged about 1,000 per year; in the mid-twentieth century it averaged about 450 per year, and by the last decade of the twentieth century about 45 per year, according to the MSHA (Szymanski 2005). The decreasing numbers of fatalities is a result of safety regulations as well as the dramatic decrease in the number of mining jobs remaining in the United States.

In the early twenty-first century, many of the mining officials appointed on the federal level were linked to the mining industry, which also resulted in the decline of fines imposed for safety infractions. John J. Sweeny, president of the AFL-CIO (from 1995 to 2009) reported that the MSHA has relaxed health and safety regulations: "17 proposed health and safety rules were withdrawn; other regulations favored by industry were implemented; and MSHA failed to keep up with existing mine safety technologies that could have saved lives in recent mining disasters" (Szymanski 2005). In the wake of the Sago Mine explosion in West Virginia on 2 January 2006, which trapped thirteen miners, of which only one survived, the UMWA reported over two hundred violations recorded at the mine since 1995. In 2005 the mine received ninety-six severe MSHA citations, and was charged less than $150 for each violation (Szymanski 2005).

While fatalities have decreased significantly, much of the hardships and lack of safety regulations and poor compensation has been offshored to other developing nations. Much like the Lattimer massacre, as well as the several union-led victories in 1900 and 1902, workers in developing countries protest, sometimes with fatal results, in an attempt to better their lives. Following are two cases that made international headlines, although with very little coverage in the United States.

Lonmin's Marikana Platinum Mine, South Africa

Protests and Violence

Lonmin PLC is registered in London with operational headquarters in Johannesburg, South Africa. Its operations focus on extracting platinum, and it is one of the three largest producers of platinum in the word, making a profit in 2011 of $158 million. The platinum mines at Marikana are near the city of Rustenberg in the northeast quadrant of South Africa, about seventy miles north of Cape Town. Like the Lattimer massacre, Lonmin's Marikana strike in South Africa in 2012 led to the death of approximately forty-seven people over several incidents, with at least an additional seventy-eight injuries reported (Nielson 2012). The event at Marikana marks the single most lethal use of force by South African security forces against civilians since 1960, during the apartheid regime. As a reaction to this event, other mines across South Africa closed as workers went on strike for better wages and living conditions. In 2012, more protests were held in South Africa than at the end of apartheid. Anna Badcock and Robert Johnston (2013, 322–23) note that one avenue of protest can begin with polite debate and move to confrontation, heckling, and assaulting police. Once in prison, passive resistance can take the form of refusing food. Protest draws attention to issues, and the demonstrator is a political actor. The demonstrator works to make visible the institutions they challenge and make visible alternative views.

The protest began with a wildcat strike at Lonmin's Marikana platinum mine on 10 August 2012. About three thousand workers walked off the job, insisting on an increase of wages to R 12,500 per month, in effect tripling their salaries (from about $500 to $1,500). Lonmin failed to meet with the strikers as they demanded wages that would lift them out of poverty. The corporation had significant control over the wages, since unemployment ranged at around 40 percent in the region. In general, the workers were exasperated with the living conditions, inequality, and poverty. Frustrated further because of a lack of progress by their union, the workers initially rejected the long-term leadership of the National Union Mineworkers (NUM) in favor of the militant Association of Mineworkers and Construction Union (AMCU). The strike gained international attention after several violent incidents between the South African Police Service, the corporation's security force, and the striking workers, which initially led to ten deaths, including miners, police officers, and mine security staff (De Wet 2012; Laing 2012; Tabane 2012). The first two miners were killed on 11 August, when the striking miners marched toward the NUM office and were fired upon by the union office. Between 12 and 14 August, violence erupted again, and four miners, two police officers, and two security guards were killed. Ignoring calls from the corporation to end the strike, the workers continued their holdout as they fought for greater than poverty wages.

The accounts of the next tragic episode, on 16 August 2012, vary greatly when comparing the different perspectives and their relationship to the event. Police said that some of the protesters were photographed from a police helicopter performing witchcraft, known as *muti*, which involved being anointed with special potions by a *sangoma*, or witch doctor, to give themselves courage in the heat of battle and make them immune to bullets (Fletcher 2012).

The police broke up striking workers who were occupying a hilltop near the Nkaneng shack settlement, and a riot erupted (Laing 2012). Riots are moments of unorganized violent disorder. Riots are generally short, unplanned episodes of violence (Dixon 2013, 564). The police could not control the crowd with tear gas, water cannons, and barbed wire, and what followed is now known as the Marikana massacre. A group of strikers came close to the police line, and the police responded by firing live rounds into the crowd for about three minutes (Illustration 5.1). In this incident the police killed thirty-four strikers and wounded at least seventy-eight others (De Wet 2012; Laing 2012; Tabane 2012).

From this point, journalists' accounts of the incident vary. BBC News reported that the strikers were holding clubs and machetes and rushed the police line. The *Times* reported that the police did not use live ammunition until they were rushed. The *Sowetan* reported that it was a peaceful gathering. *Al Jazeera* reported that the police in armored vehicles forced the strikers into an area surrounded by razor wire and then began shooting (SAPA 2012b).

Though South Africa became a democratic nation eighteen years earlier, the killings by the police force was a reminder of apartheid. Most people could not believe that the extent of the brutality by the state police force could equal the carnage of the apartheid regime. Even more striking is that this incident was perpetrated by a police force under the oversight of the ANC government, which fought against this type of police brutality (Fletcher 2012).

An archaeology of protest may highlight hidden and repressed voices and reveal power, power of the past, present, and potentially the future (Badcock and Johnston 2013, 333). A postmortem examination contradicts the police account that they fired upon an attacking mob. The au-

Illustration 5.1. Police advance after shooting striking workers with live ammunition on 16 August 2012. "Marikana Massacre 16 August 2012," South African History, online, www.sahistory.org.za http://www.sahistory.org.za/article/marikana-massacre-16-august-2012.

topsy report of the dead indicates that the majority of the strikers were shot in the back while fleeing the confrontation, and many were shot far from the police line. Fourteen of the miners were shot over three hundred meters away from the police line. Only one handgun was found among the strikers. A reporter for the *Daily Maverick*, Greg Marinovich, examined the scene and found that a group of victims appeared to have been cornered and shot at close range. If they were shot from farther away he would have found a shower of bullets throughout the area. However, few stray bullets were found, suggesting that once they were cornered, the police closed in on them and shot them at close range, producing few stray shots. "It is becoming clear to this reporter that heavily armed police hunted down and killed the miners in cold blood" (Marinovich 2012; see also Liang 2012). Zweli Mnisi, spokesman for the local police minister, condemned the report as "irresponsible" (quoted in Liang 2012). Shortly after the massacre, the national police commissioner, General Riah Phiyega, noted that she authorized the use of live ammunition because "the militant group stormed towards the police firing shots and wielding dangerous weapons" (quoted in Liang 2012).

The day after the shootings a group of miners' wives protested. They sang and chanted slogans from the antiapartheid movement. They also chanted anti-police songs. They insisted that the police officers responsible for the shooting be fired, and they demanded to know what had happened to their husbands—referring to those 270 miners that were arrested. One protest banner read, "Police, stop shooting our husbands and sons" (BBC News 2012b).

Over twenty-eight thousand miners remained on strike in mid-September, even though the company said that those who did not show for work would be dismissed. The deadline to return to work passed and the workers continued to strike. Wildcat strikes spread throughout South Africa. South African president Jacob Zuma sent a military convoy to the area, and on 15 September, the demonstrations again turned violent. The police fired tear gas on protesters in a shanty town. Two days later another protester was shot by police (*Al Jazeera* 2012b).

By the end of September 2012, the company and the workers resolved their wage dispute with the help of the South African Council of Churches, along with the moderate union NUM and the exclusion of the AMCU. A minimum entry wage was established, to be enacted within two years. Miners received a 22 percent pay raise and a oneoff payment of R 2,000, and in exchange, they would return to work on 20 September 2012 (*Al Jazeera* 2012a; De Wet 2012; iAfrica 2012). However, labor clashes continued elsewhere, such as at the Anglo American Platinum (Amplats) mine. These miners demanded a similar wage increase. When the protesters blocked roads, the police fired tear gas and stun grenades to disperse the strikers (*Al Jazeera* 2012a; McClenaghan 2012). The Marikana massacre created significant concerns about the ability of the ANC under Zuma to improve the lives of those who had been suppressed for so long—poor black South Africans (BBC News 2012b).

Immediately after the Marikana massacre, 270 miners were arrested and detained by the police. First, they were charged with public violence, and then later with thirty-four counts of murder, a similar tactic used by the former apartheid government. The idea that those imprisoned were charged with killing their fellow strikers was incongruous with the democratic leadership of the ANC. On 2 September, the National Prosecuting Authority announced that they would drop the murder charges against the miners, who were eventually released over the next several days (De Waal 2012).

Those miners who were captured and imprisoned later filed over 150 complaints that they were tortured while in police custody (De Wet 2012; Laing 2012; Tabane 2012). Some claimed that those held prisoner were beaten with batons and fists in order to implicate their colleagues in the killing of two police officers in the initial skirmish (BBC News 2012c). A resident of Marikana and mine worker noted, "They make us stand out and they search us again. They say we must not look at them. Other of us they made us take off our clothes." Another miner said that he was made to stand against the wall with his hands above his head. Then the police beat him in the ribs with their bare hands and a stick. Others were slapped and had their fingers stomped on with boots (Hlongwane 2012). The South African justice system is a long way from reforming. For instance, in 2010, there were 1,769 cases of people dying in police custody, and about 5,000 cases of assault, torture, and other misconduct by police (Nielson 2012).

The Judicial Inquiry

President Jacob Zuma ordered a judicial inquiry to investigate the violence and report back to him by January (*Al Jazeera* 2012c). Retired judge Ian Farlam was charged with establishing the cause of the killing of the thirty-four striking workers and the wounding of seventy-eight others (SAPA 2012c). When the hearings began, "family members of miners shot and killed at the Lonmin Platinum mine collapsed and broke into loud sobs as video footage of the shooting was shown to the judicial commission of inquiry on Tuesday" (SAPA 2012c). While a number of women wailed and collapsed to the floor, others began to scream and shout, and others were carried out of the room (SAPA 2012c). At the Farlam commission hearing, a local community leader expressed her frustration with Lonmin because they did not keep their obligation to better the living conditions of the traditional community—the Bapo Ba Mogale. The mining charter notes that the company has socioeconomic obligations, which included infrastructure and job creation in the area. Many of the miners live in single-sex hostels where "workers are stacked in bunks like so many artifacts in a museum" (SAPA 2012c). Many put up with the conditions out of desperation, living in poverty conditions, because unemployment runs very high (McClenaghan 2012). "Lonmin is exploiting minerals that belong to the royal family and its traditional community," the community member explained (SAPA 2012c).

Dumisa Ntsebeza, who served as advocate for several families of the miners killed, told the Farlam commission that the police acted as though the miners were "possessed vermin" who "had to be destroyed like vermin" and "were killed like vermin" (quoted in Toisi 2012). Another advocate for the miners described the police's actions as "acts of revenge" for the two policemen killed several days before the massacre (quoted in Toisi 2012). Some of the evidence was falsified by the police. For instance, in one photograph, a dead man was lying on rocky ground near the mine. A second picture of the same scene taken several hours later had a yellow-handled machete under the man's right hand. There are also photographs of miners who lay dead with handcuffs on (BBC News 2012a).

The Bench Marks Foundation responded to this situation in October 2012, with a document entitled "What Government Needs to Do to Prevent Another Marikana." The foundation is an independent nonprofit, faithbased organization owned by the churches in South Africa. It is part of an international faithbased coalition that has partners around the world. Its aim is to monitor multinational corporations so that they implement socially responsible policies. The Bench Marks Foundation (2012) clearly states that its goal is to monitor these corporations to ensure:

- They respect human rights;
- They protect the environment;
- That profitmaking is not done at the expense of other interest groups; and
- That those most negatively impacted upon are heard, protected, and accommodated within the business plans of the corporations.

The foundation explained that the discontent that arose from the Marikana strike will not go away until the root causes are addressed. The foundation also noted that the company's high profits were at the expense of low wages for the workers. The exploitation of these workers was the main cause of the violence. The Bench Marks Foundation reported, "The benefits of mining are not reaching the workers or the surrounding communities. Lack of employment opportunities for local youth, squalid living conditions, unemployment and growing inequalities contribute to this mess" (SAPA 2012a). Every day the miners face falling rocks, exposure to dust, intensive noise, fumes, and high temperatures, among others (ILO 2012). Jo Seoka, chairman of the Bench Marks Foundation, noted that the community living near the mine was not benefiting from the corporation's profits. He explained, "Corporations, often with the support of government leaders, make very large profits while communities suffer high levels of inequality and poverty. The situation in Marikana testifies to this" (SAPA 2012c).

The Bench Marks Foundation document made recommendations directed not only to mining companies, but also to government, parliament, and other state bodies as well as civil society and communities. The government lacked a credible response to Marikana, dealing with the unrest in the most forceful way (Bench Marks Foundation 2012). John Capel, executive director of the Bench Marks Foundation, stated, "We need to ask why such a forceful response was taken." Capel notes, "It begs the question in whose interests was government's response to Marikana directed to?" Capel explained that there exists a conflict of interest among companies and politicians. For instance, mining companies can lobby politicians, and politicians are allowed to participate as board members for companies or as shareholders. Therefore, the Bench Marks Foundation concluded that the involvement of government officials in mining companies undermines democracy (Bench Marks Foundation 2012).

The foundation also noted that while private companies operate to maximize profits to increase shareholder returns, there is a lot more that corporations can do to improve the situation for communities. Capel said, "Regardless of what they say, mining is a profitable business and we need to ensure that all involved benefit from it. . . . Government has the power to make a huge impact. The question is: does it have the will to do so?" (Bench Marks Foundation 2012).

Nearly a year later, the Farlam commission announced on 20 September 2013 that the police version of the event "is in material respects not the truth" (*Washington Post* 2013). The commission proclaimed that the police officers lied and withheld information.

A progressive magazine wrote:

> Perhaps the most important lesson of Marikana is that the state can gun down dozens of black workers with little or no backlash from "civil society," the judicial system or from within the institutions that supposedly form the bedrock of democracy. What we have instead is the farcical Farlam commission, an obvious attempt to clear the state's role in the massacre and prevent any sort of real investigation into the actions of the police on that day. In other words, the state can get away with mass murder, with apparent impunity in terms of institutional conceptions of justice and political accountability. (Fogel 2013)

Memorialization

Two years after the Marikana massacre, different forms of memorialization to remember the event developed throughout South Africa. In Cape Town, for one day, the street name signs had a second street name erected underneath them, almost the same size as the original street name. For example, on Parliament Street, the name Molefi Osiel Ntsoele Street was placed under the official street name for the day. Molefi Ntsoele was one of the thirty-four miners killed at Marikana. He was from the mountain village of Ha Tebesi in Lesotho and was employed as a rock driller. He made the long journey home every two weeks to bring groceries to his family. He was killed by police on 16 August 2012 at Marikana. There were thirty-three other street signs with the names of those killed throughout Cape Town. Near each sign was a short biography of each miner and a photograph (Davis 2014).

Also in Cape Town, several statues of colonial figures were dressed in mining overalls and a miner's head lamp. Banners with protest slogans were found throughout the city. A miner's face, was illuminated by a torch, had the words:

> The right to life.
> The right to a living wage.
> The struggle continues . . . (Davis 2014)

A graffiti stencil with the slogan "Remember Marikana" appeared in blood-red paint on walls, buildings, road signs, and bus stops around Cape Town. The collective responsible for the graffiti noted, "We want to remind people both of this atrocity and the fact that people remain resolute and indignant in spite of it" (Davis 2014). The Marikana stencil was also applied to the Cecil John Rhodes statue on the University of Cape Town campus. While the University of Cape Town called the stencil an act of vandalism and an insult, others saw it as a reminder of the connection between colonialism and the long history of dispossession and exploitation and the murder of poor black people (Davis 2014).

Other forms of remembering the Marikana victims have been sanctioned by the African Arts Institute (AFAI). The organization sponsored a display of photographs in Church Square of the women and children of Marikana. The AFAI also organized a mural painting of a miner in Nyanga. In Langa, the AFAI hosted two screenings of the documentary *Miners Shot Down*, followed by a public debate. On the anniversary date, seven poets walked the streets of central Cape Town along with thirty-four actors representing the miners killed. Jill Williams of the AFAI commented, "It was a performance art piece, like a poetic ritual, but in the form of a group mourning through the city" (Davis 2014).

Soma Mine, Turkey
Disaster in a Coal Mine

Mine disasters with high fatality rates were common in Western Europe and the United States as the mining industry developed in the nineteenth century until the industry gained strong union representation in the early twentieth century. It still remains a dangerous occupation into the twenty-first century with primary (fires and cave-ins) and secondary (silicosis) occupational threats. While the fatality rate has decreased in the Western hemisphere, occupational threats are significantly higher in developing countries, where resource extraction is important for the local and national economies. In order to ensure profitability, corporations consistently pursue cost-cutting measures, and as a result there is also a rise in the fatality rate. While China consistently has one of the highest mortality rates related to mining, the Soma disaster in Turkey in 2014 is considered one of the worst coal mining disasters of the twenty-first century (Craighill 2014).

The world's coal mines supply about 30 percent of global energy needs (Berkes 2014). Coal mining is a major industry in the Soma area in western Turkey, helping to supply a nearby lignite-fired thermal power plant. Nearly 40 percent of Turkey's electricity production depends on coal (BBC News 2014c). During the liberalization of the electricity market in Turkey in 2002, the government began auctioning off coalfield operating licenses to private companies. There were no conditions, no audits, and no government regulations, with the goal of making all the coal resources available for mining as soon as possible (Craighill 2014).

Coal mining is responsible for the highest proportion of fatalities of any other energy source production due to poor working conditions in countries such as China, Turkey, South Africa, Indonesia, and Colombia. The Soma disaster is one of the worst incidents in a sector that has experienced thirty thousand known deaths since 1970 (Thornhill 2014). Turkey has poor mine safety conditions, and accidents leading to injuries and deaths are common. "The risk is constant . . . and the margins of error are low," explained Tom Hethmon, a professor of mine safety at the University of Utah and a consultant to international mining companies (quoted in Berkes 2014). A 2010 report by the Turkish Economy Policies Research Foundation (TEPAV) noted that the fatality rate in the Turkey coal mining industry was five times higher than China, a country known for its high fatality rate. Turkey's mining fatality rate began to increase after the privatization of the mines. Recent trade union experts noted that there has been a 40 percent increase in mine accidents since privatization (Kotsev 2014). In 2014, there were 1,886 industry-related deaths in Turkey, up from 878 in 2012, according the Turkish Assembly for Workers' Health (Lowen 2015). Regarding mining fatalities in particular, about three thousand miners have died in accidents since 1941. Mahmut Arslan, chairman of the pro-Islamic Hak-Is workers' confederation, said that "eighty per cent of these could have been avoided if necessary safety measures had been taken." He noted that "the priority is not safety but profitability" (*Economist* 2014). According to the International Labor Organization, Turkey has recently averaged one hundred mine fatalities a year. After twenty-nine miners died in 2010 in Massey Energy's Upper Big Branch mine in West Virginia, the US average for fatalities hovered around twenty deaths in 2012 and 2013, while China has more than one thousand fatalities annually (Berkes 2014). In 2012, the International Labor Organization ranked Turkey third worst in the world for worker deaths (Vick 2014). In 2011, workplace accidents in Turkey were 15.4 per hundred thousand workers, compared to 2.6 in the twenty-eight EU countries. Mine accidents represent a significant proportion of those deaths in Turkey (Human Rights Watch 2015).

Soma is a town of about one hundred thousand residents, and its only economy is coal. Many of the miners are from agricultural villages. Their community's traditional livelihoods in farming and livestock have suffered, and many of the men have turned to mining in order to support their families (Yeginsu 2015). A board member of the Soma chamber of commerce noted, "There are no other jobs here. If you don't work in the mine, you trade coal. It's all there is here" (quoted in Letsch 2014). By the end of 2013, miners were protesting against the dangerous mining conditions and the lack of the enforcement of safety regulations. On 29 April 2014, the main opposition party, the Republican People's Party (CHP), demanded an investigation of mine safety. The petition was rejected by the Grand National Assembly of Turkey. They reasoned that the Labor Ministry inspected the Soma mines in March 2014, and it passed inspection. Yet Ozgur Ozel, a deputy from the CHP, said that he was being swamped by complaints about the safety conditions in the mines, and he asked for another inspection. His request was rejected by the then prime minister, Recep Tayyip Erdoğan's, Justice and Development Party (AKP) (*Economist* 2014).

Coal mines are volatile places. Coal seams contain explosive methane gas and coal dust, an accelerant that feeds explosions. Soma mining continued during the shift change, so for a period of time workers from both shifts are underground at the same time. While this practice enhances productivity, it also doubles the risk of fatalities (Berkes 2014). On 13 May 2014, there was an explosion in a coal mine in Soma about two kilometers below the surface. The explosion and fire occurred at a shift change, and 787 miners were underground at the time. The fire burned for two days. The explosion originated in a power distribution center, which brings electricity to the mine. Every power center and cable as well as mining machines are potential sources of ignition. An ignition can trigger methane and coal dust explosions. Four mine rescue teams were sent to the site (Illustration 5.2). The explosion cut power, and the elevators could not carry survivors out of the mines. When the elevators stopped working, rescue crews pumped fresh air into the mines, but survivors of the explosion were overcome by noxious gases (Berkes 2014). Authorities said that most deaths were caused by carbon monoxide poisoning (Thornhill 2014).

Two days after the extinguishing of the fire, all of the bodies were removed. The final count was 301 miners killed in the fatal accident, with

Illustration 5.2. Rescue operation in progress at the Soma mine disaster in Turkey. Image by Mustafa Karaman, https://en.wikipedia.org/wiki/Soma_mine_disaster#/media/File:Soma_mine_disaster12.JPG.

most of them succumbing to carbon monoxide poisoning. An additional 162 men were injured. It was Turkey's worst industrial disaster and the world's biggest mining disaster this century. While the mining company claimed that the accident was unforeseen, it was a result of a relatively unregulated industry with profit-focused goals that cut corners on safety procedures (Craighill 2014; Human Rights Watch 2015).

The Immediate Reaction

The large-scale fatality rate impacted just about every family in the community. The Turkish government announced three days of national mourning for the Soma miners. The mining company, Soma Kömür İşletmeleri AŞ, replaced the company website with a black page as a message of condolence (Watson et al. 2014). Protests erupted throughout the nation, including in Istanbul, Ankara, İzmir, and Zonguldak. In Ankara, about eight hundred people tried to march from the Middle East Technical University (METU) to the Ministry of Energy and Natural Resources. The crowd threw stones at police and shouted anti-government slogans. Hundreds also protested outside of the company headquarters located in Istanbul. Some sprayed the word "Murderers" on the building's wall (BBC

News 2014c; *Guardian* 2014; Lamparski et al. 2014). Security forces used tear gas and water cannons against twenty thousand protesters in İzmir (Letsch 2014). On 15 May, Turkey's largest trade union, Turk-Is, which consisted of eight hundred thousand workers, joined a one-day strike as unions demanded better working conditions (Thornhill 2014). In Istanbul, a group chanted anti-government slogans and carried a large banner that read, "It's not an accident, it's murder" (Thornhill 2014).

Several unions participated in a twenty-four-hour strike. They blamed the privatization of the mining sector, which made working conditions more dangerous. In the streets of Ankara, about three thousand people marched (BBC News 2014c). Demonstrators wearing miner's helmets gathered outside the Istanbul headquarters of the mining company. On subway platforms some commuters pretended to be dead (Vick 2014).

Turkey's minister for energy and natural resources, Taner Yildiz, made it clear that he accepted the human cost involved for profit. In an attempt to console the community, he stated, "We are moving toward the worst mining disaster in Turkey," and then later stated that the "death toll figures are not important" (Erimtan 2014). Prime Minister Erdoğan (now president of Turkey) visited Soma the day after the disaster to survey the site of the mining disaster, and at a press conference tried to ease the pain of loss. Instead, he inflamed the Turkish public by explaining, "I went back in British history. Some 204 people died there after a mine collapsed in 1838. In 1866, 361 miners died in Britain. In an explosion in 1894, 290 people died there. Take America with all of its technology and everything . . . In 1907, 361 [miners died there]." He then concluded by stating "these are usual things" (Erimtan 2014). Erdoğan did not gauge the anger of the mourning community. His car was surrounded by hundreds of people as a response to his statements. As Erdoğan walked through Soma, onlookers showered him with deafening jeers as well as chants of "Resign, Prime Minister!" (Tuysuz and Smith-Spark 2014). When he emerged from his car he was chased through the city, and he took refuge in a shop. People began throwing rocks and shouting that the prime minister was a murderer and a thief (BBC News 2014a, 2014b).

Erdoğan's aide, Yusuf Yerkel, captured public attention when he was photographed standing over a fallen protester, kicking him. The image became a symbol of how the working class felt it was treated and also of how the privileged administration treated dissent. A picture also appeared showing the prime minister slapping a protester (BBC News 2014c). Generally, Erdoğan and his staff were criticized for being insensitive to the needs of the community and the mourning nation by suggesting that the disaster was a fact of life (BBC News 2014c).

Most of the town's inhabitants are conservative working-class voters who are a major part of Erdoğan's support base. However, when he said that accidents were inevitable in the mining industry, the community's anger grew. "Our mourning is starting to turn into anger," one member of the regional miners' union said. "What does the prime minister mean when he says such things? It is time for the government to admit their mistakes, to stand behind us. Instead they come here and laugh at our pain" (quoted in Letsch 2014). One retired miner whose son died in the disaster stated, "The prime minister called the accident fate, said it was in the nature of the job, but they won't make any of us see it that way." "It was a massacre. It could have been prevented, and the state is protecting itself" (quoted in Human Rights Watch 2015).

In Soma, protesters dressed mostly in black and chanted, "Don't sleep, Soma, remember you're dead!" as they passed through city streets a few miles from the disaster site trying to reach a statue honoring miners (Tuysuz and Smith-Spark 2014). Police used tear gas, plastic pellets, and a water cannon on protesters angered by the government's response (Tuysuz and Smith-Spark 2014). Local authorities banned protests in Soma, and several dozen were detained (Tuysuz and Smith-Spark 2014).

President Abdullah Gül came to Soma after Erdoğan's visit. Gül went to the hospital where the injured were taken, and he also went to the scene of the disaster. He called on all Turks to be "unified . . . to get over these hard times" (BBC News 2014c). His visit did not create the stir that was caused by Prime Minister Erdoğan, although he was heckled by crowds. "Why does he come here with an army of police and security personnel?" asked one angry miner who did not want to be named. "These people come here with their nice suits and their ties, but no compassion for our suffering" (quoted in Letsch 2014). Another responded, "They don't put any value on a human life. All they care about is profit, and nothing else" (quoted in Letsch 2014). One woman who works in a government office in Soma and has a son who works in the mines said she was tired of the government's attitude. "They are lying to us. This was no accident. This was murder, plain and simple" (quoted in Letsch 2014).

Lack of Worker Safety

Before the incident, the Soma mining company's CEO boasted that he had lowered the cost of extracting coal from $140/ton to $24/ton, and doubled the output; however, it is apparent that this increased profit came at the expense of safety regulations. A report submitted by experts to the Soma Public Prosecutor's Office in September 2014 cited poor ventilation, gas masks that did not function, the absence of gas sensors and rescue chambers, and the presence of overly flammable equipment, among other lapses (Human Rights Watch 2015; Yenginsu 2015). The transformer that exploded was made locally, and perhaps not made to code (Lowen 2015).

One miner noted the extreme pressure to produce. "When I once complained about the heat to the chief, he just said, 'Is there coal on the conveyor belt, is there output? Forget the rest.' I spent more time crawling on the ground through those narrow passages on my belly than I did during military service. I used to get very angry sometimes about the pressure we were put under. The chiefs were given incentives to produce more, but we didn't see the benefits" (quoted in Human Rights Watch 2015). A safety officer in the mine explained how rules were not enforced:

> There was continually pressure from above so that they would never agree to stopping work to fix things, as it would have interrupted production... On paper there were safety standards but they were never implemented. For instance, a sign saying "Don't clean the conveyor belt while operating" hung by the conveyor belt, but we always had to clean it while it was operating because the company never wanted to halt production. (Quoted in Human Rights Watch 2015)

One miner reported that the gas masks were never inspected, repaired, or replaced. "In 2010 there was a fire at the mine as a result of an electrical fault," he said. "We had to use the gas masks and half of them turned out not to work." During the May 2014 fire, some masks failed to be effective against the carbon monoxide (Human Rights Watch 2015).

One Year Later

A criminal investigation showed that the miners were working in dangerous conditions. Miners also described the ineffective inspections, the lack of implementing safety standards, and the lack of adequate safety equipment. The company ignored warnings of elevated firedamp levels and rising heat (Human Rights Watch 2015).

As a result of the Soma tragedy, in September 2014, the Turkish parliament passed a law to improve working conditions in mining, and in March 2015, Turkey ratified the International Labor Organization Safety and Health in Mines Convention (no. 176) (Human Rights Watch 2015). Mining companies are mandated to install oxygen mask stations, tracking systems for miners, emergency rooms, and other safety measures, while companies that neglect workers' safety now face harsher fines and bans from public tenders (*Daily Sabah* 2016).

Emma Sinclair-Webb, a senior Turkey researcher at Human Rights Watch, explains that a trial of the company's mine employees may offer a chance to achieve justice. At the same time, the trial does not address the government's failure to protect the mine workers. She noted, "The government's role in the Soma disaster needs to be investigated and corrected if Turkey is going to be able to reverse its terrible record of preventable mine accidents" (quoted in Human Rights Watch 2015).

Prosecutors want to hold the state inspectors and other civil servants responsible for the death of the miners, claiming that officials failed to provide appropriate safety oversight. Prosecution of civil servants and public officials (under law no. 4483) can only occur after securing administrative permission, underscoring that the offenses were committed in the course of their public duties. According to Human Rights Watch (2015), law no. 4483 is contrary to Turkey's human rights obligations. The minister of labor and social security and the minister of energy and natural resources have the power to refuse permission for a criminal investigation that could lead to the criminal prosecution of state officials (Human Rights Watch 2015). In December 2014, Faruk Çelik, the labor and social security minister, said that the ministry would conduct its own administrative investigation into two employees instead of agreeing to a criminal investigation, and contended that the disaster was the result of the mine's outdated structure (Human Rights Watch 2015).

The trial of fifty-one mining company employees and engineers began in April 2015, in a cultural center in the town of Akhisar. Eight defendants, including the chief executive and the general manager of the mine company in Soma, faced voluntary manslaughter charges. Hundreds of relatives of the deceased marched through the town demanding harsh sentences. Some wore mining helmets painted black and carrying the names of the deceased (Human Rights Watch 2015; *Guardian* 2015). The eight executives and managers operating the mine faced multiple life sentences if found guilty. An additional forty-three managers faced up to fifteen years in prison for similar but lesser charges (*Daily Sabah* 2016; Toksabay and Gumrukcu 2018).

The pro-Kurdish Peoples' Democratic Party leader, Selahattin Demirtas, noted, "There is not a single politician sitting in the defendants' seats. Justice can never be fully delivered unless the court takes into account the responsibility of politicians" (*Guardian* 2015). The community continues to be disappointed by the response of the government and President Erdoğan. "They promised us compensation, a house and jobs, but we've seen nothing," said one widow. Another noted, "What has he done since? Built himself a palace and left us here to hopelessly drown in our sorrows," referring to the $600 million presidential palace that opened in Ankara in October 2014 (Yeginsu 2015). The widows of the Soma mining disaster support their families with their husbands' life insurance stipends. One community member lost her two sons, and she receives the equivalent of $370 a month as a result of her sons' pensions. "But nobody from the government has visited us, nobody has come to see how we are. I feel betrayed. I used to vote for the [governing] AK Party, but never again" (Lowen 2015). Each family was also promised $83,000 in compensation, but a year after the tragedy, none had been paid (Yeginsu 2015).

A year after the disaster, many claimed that they continued to have feelings of hopelessness and depression. Some had difficulty sleeping and had a loss of interest in life (Human Rights Watch 2015). The wife of a miner who died said, "I want to see the state take responsibility for this. Our children are without fathers. I have little confidence in justice in Turkey. As well as my husband last year, seven years ago I lost my brother in a mine accident. No one got a prison sentence. And my aunt's husband also died in a mine accident before that. There is never justice here" (quoted in Human Rights Watch 2015).

The families associated with the Soma disaster feel that justice remains elusive. At the first anniversary of the disaster, protest rallies were held in the Soma region. People dressed as miners, and others carried the photographs and names of the miners who died. The protesters chanted "Erdoğan: thief, murderer" and "The coal of Soma will burn down the government" (Lowen 2015). One protester remarked, "This is not an accident, it's murder. As long as this government remains, there can be no justice" (quoted in Lowen 2015). "To call it an accident is sinful—it was coldblooded murder," said a miner's widow from Koseler (quoted in Yeginsu 2015). One bereaved widow explained, "We never had much, but we had each other, and we were happy. Every day without him feels like a different kind of hell" (quoted in Yeginsu 2015).

A spokesman for the Ministry of Labor said the government had delivered on all of its promises after the disaster. "We are paying monthly compensation to the families of the victims and have adopted a new law to improve conditions for miners and amend security regulations," he said. "Any additional compensation is the responsibility of the mining company" (quoted in Yenginsu 2015).

Turkey paid about $8 million to the surviving workers and families of victims, as well as salary support for six months, and designated monthly payments for those workers who die in occupational accidents. The government also offered public sector jobs to the relatives of the victims, as part of efforts to help families in which deceased workers were often the sole breadwinners for their households (*Daily Sabah* 2016). Some widows of the mining disaster are now working for low wages with the goal of pooling their money so that their children can receive an education and not work in the mines (Yeginsu 2015).

In the nearby mining community of Elmadere, many of the villagers are selling their land to the new Polyak Eynez coal mine. They typically receive the equivalent of one year's pay for a coal miner. However, since the Soma incident, the families of the men killed at Soma are not selling to the company. They explain that they will not support the industry that killed their family members (Yeginsu 2015).

On the second anniversary of the Soma accident, local officials and lawmakers attended an official commemoration ceremony. Relatives of the victims came to the Soma Mine Martyrs' Cemetery. Some mourned out loud, weeping and crying, while others recited the Quran and prayers. Some children left drawings for their late fathers (*Daily Sabah* 2016).

Turkey continues to have a poor mining safety record, as hundreds of miners are killed by accidents each year. In 2014, as a result of the Soma disaster, the government created stricter work safety rules, which include financial penalties and prison terms for those found liable in fatal accidents. In 2018, a Turkish court sentenced the Soma mining company's general manager and technical manager to twenty-two years in prison. Two other company officials were sentenced to nearly nineteen years, and the chairman was sentenced to fifteen years in prison. The court sentenced nine other employees to shorter jail terms, and acquitted the remaining defendants, who had faced charges ranging from "killing with probable intent" to "criminally negligent manslaughter" (Toksabay and Gumrukcu 2018).

Conclusion

The coal operators of northeastern Pennsylvania became prisoners of their own mythology. Improvements, such as ventilation shafts and second exits and miner's hospitals, were seen as humanitarian and costly safety measures. The coal operator placed these expenses in a mental account separate from the day-to-day operations of the mine. To begin developing safety regulations and implement safety measures would be an admission of previous unsafe practices and would serve as a precedent in a court case. However, not developing safety practices not only killed many workers, but also slowed production and created many bankruptcies (Wallace 1987). However, places like Marikana and Soma are reminders of common work and labor practices in nineteenth-century Western Europe and the United States. The greed to produce more at the expense of human life and welfare led to fatal tragedies in the past. In developing countries today these conditions persist, as resource extraction and the associated exploitation has become common in places that depend on the resources for the development of their economy.

CONCLUSION

Difficult Histories Are a Reality in the Present

Difficult Histories Are Present

Randall McGuire reminds us that, "What we choose to remember, what we choose to study, what questions we ask, and how we frame the answers all have political importance for identity, heritage, social agency and fast capitalism . . . we should make these decisions in a conscious praxis of archaeology" (McGuire 2008, 235). Therefore, it is important that the focus of inequality in the workplace be expanded in our civic discourse, including when addressing issues related to the continuous abuses of unchecked capitalism. Memorializing working-class history is one way to ensure that debate surrounding these issues continues and becomes more prominent in our public memory (Little and Shackel 2014; Roller 2018a, 2018b; Shackel 2009, 2018a; Smith et al. 2011).

Archaeology can help preserve the memory of a place and bring a forgotten place back to the public memory. Archaeology can help recover memory as well as produce landscapes of counter memory (González-Ruibal 2008, 251). By focusing on the destructive processes of unchecked capitalism, archaeology can be a critical voice in understanding the conditions of the contemporary world. Examining deindustrialization, labor strife, and the ruined landscape provides an avenue to discover and re-evaluate a forgotten and sometimes hidden history. The knowledge produced by our archaeologies can be part of the political struggle about the past as well as the present. Therefore, a glimpse into the national and the international provides a vehicle to discerning alternative histories.

For instance, a large proportion of the northeastern Pennsylvania anthracite landscape is in ruins from abandoned mining and forgotten, abandoned, and partially abandoned towns. Some ruins can be treated as objects that should not be disturbed, thereby creating an explicit sense of a past. However, that only occurs if there is a consensus, a type of official public memory that allows for the commemoration and sanctification of ruins. In the case of these ruined landscapes, created by abandonment or disasters, the goal is to create an anti-memory to remove and clean these disasters away from the public memory. It is only through subversive means that they become memorialized through smaller acts of remembrance, acts that may not last ad infinitum. Protests, commemorative services, and street signs last for a while; however, they are not anchored in a more lasting general commemoration (Shackel 2016, 2018b).

Visitors to northeastern Pennsylvania began describing the environmental destruction in this region soon after the American Civil War, and the environmental degradation continued well into the twentieth century. Many of the natural resources have been compromised, and it is common to find many miles of dead streams in the region from acid mine drainage. Industries that employed children and women, like silk mills and cigar factories, sit abandoned on the landscape, slowly decaying. In the 1960s, geographers (Deasy and Griess 1961; Griess and Deasy 1964) noted the potential in developing tourism focusing on deindustrialization and environmental degradation. They described the place as the badlands of industrial ruins, a curiosity much like the slums of Paris. Today, urban explorers come to the region to visit the abandoned breakers and derelict factories, as well as to view the remains of Centralia, a town slowly being abandoned because of an underground mine fire that began in the early 1960s and will continue to burn for several hundred years.

Tim Strangleman (2013, 33) argues that ruins can be a place of "uncritical sentimentalization of the past, one where tensions of gender and race, if not always class, go unnoticed, one where the destructive impacts of industry on health and environment are obscured." The ruins on the northeastern Pennsylvania landscape serve as a reminder of the industrial past and the structural violence encountered by the new immigrants. The long-term effects of the structural violence continue to affect the contemporary population. The reality of inevitable decay and destruction of industry can challenge the long-perceived notion of the benefits of capitalism (Brown 2015; Lam 2013; Smith and Campbell 2017). Scholars like Karl Marx, Joseph Schumpeter, and David Harvey have noted that capitalism must go through a destructive process to create an opening for new wealth. This form of creative destruction creates ruins at an increasing rate, which impacts humans and landscapes (Harrison and Schofield 2010). Gaston Gordillo (2014, 17) notes that these places are geographies destroyed at the altar of profit.

Joseph Schumpeter (1950) popularized the term "creative destruction" in his book *Capitalism, Socialism, and Democracy*. Presenting it as something positive depoliticizes the actions associated with this concept. Destruction is redefined as innovative, positive, and desirable. It is part of a thriving system. "It is therefore not surprising that neoliberal economists and corporate actors fully endorse the idea that capitalism is defined by creative destruction. This concept allows them to admit that capitalism is destructive, while at the same time highlighting that, in spite of this, the system creates wealth and places defined by wholeness" (Gordillo 2014, 80). The disregard for the consequences of destruction is what makes the current conditions found in these zones of destruction in the contemporary world alarming, as the impact on the environment as well as on the health and lives of the working class has been quite significant. Marshal Berman (1982, 100) wrote that the contemporary ruling class is "the most violently destructive ruling class in history."

Jefferson Cowie and Joseph Heathcott (2003, 14) also caution us that creeping industrial nostalgia threatens to erase the meaning of the consequences of deindustrialization on the economy, people, and the environment. They write that "we have to strip industrial work of its broad-shouldered, social-realist patina and see it for what it was: tough work that people did because it paid well, and it was located in their communities" (Cowie and Heathcott 2003, 15).

A ruined landscape is about job loss, health issues, and environmental degradation—in the past as well as in the present (High 2013a, 2013b; Mah 2009, 2010, 2012). Severin Fowles notes that "capitalism has not . . . learned to embrace its own ruins as legitimate spaces of reuse, reoccupation, and innovation. Modernity may promise a world that is brilliantly new, but its great irony is that it delivers more and more ruins, the study of which reminds us that modernity is always incomplete, always moving on" (Fowles 2010, 780).

Ann Stoler (2013) encourages us to think about the concept of ruination when thinking about the ruins and the industrial past. Rather than explaining ruins as creative destruction in the larger process of capitalism, ruination takes into account the social, political, and economic consequences of the destructive nature of unchecked capitalism. Ruination is what people are left with, and what remains can include the lack of decent-paying jobs, general poor health, altered landscapes, and distorted and ruined social and personal lives. The signatures of ruination are urban decay, environmental degradation, industrial pollution, and/or racialized unemployment—the refuse of a capitalist market that has since moved on (Stoler 2008, 200). It is important to recognize the people who live in these ruined landscapes, since the conditions of industry still have an impact on their daily lives today (Stoler 2013, 9). Stoler (2008, 196) explains, "Ruination is more than a process. It is also a political project that lays waste to certain peoples and places, relations, and things." She also notes that "ruination is a corrosive process that weighs on the future and shapes the present" (Stoler 2008, 194).

The concept of ruination is a way of understanding how the signatures of structural violence and historical trauma can be read on the contemporary landscape. It is important to note that the concept of ruination is a vehicle to examine how these forms of structural violence embedded in capitalism still exist, in different forms and in different geographical areas (Shackel 2018b).

Story of Textile Mills

While northeastern Pennsylvania is best known for its mining heritage, other industries did prosper in the region, even if for a short time. For instance, in the late nineteenth century, northeastern Pennsylvanian women went to work in the developing textile industry. Many textile operations came to the region fleeing organized labor in the industrial northeast. In many cases, women became the main providers of their households, especially after the collapse of the mining industry that began in the post–World War I era (Dublin 1998, 29). While the textile industry flourished for a few decades, capital once again mobilized and began its exit from northeastern Pennsylvania in the 1970s and 1980s. Textile operators fled organized labor, first moving to the American South and eventually locating offshore (Wolensky 2003).

While the coal barons and textile owners have disappeared from the region, modern corporations and their fulfillment centers have migrated to northeastern Pennsylvania and have taken their place. In general, these large distribution centers have developed in suburban and semirural areas in the United States where the average wage is low, and unemployment is relatively high. In Hazleton, Pennsylvania, a city of about twenty-five thousand people, nearly five thousand people are employed in the Keystone Opportunity Zone in mostly unskilled, low-paying jobs. Many of these jobs are in fulfillment centers. These companies control a vast amount of the region's capital, much like the coal operators did a century ago, thereby controlling the lives and livelihoods of the area's residents, including immigrants. Unskilled, low-wage jobs are the norm, and there is little infusion of new capital to revive the infrastructure of the region and improve the living conditions in these communities (Longazel 2016; Shackel 2018a).

While many textiles operations have moved offshore, reports from the US Department of State estimates that there are about one hundred thousand people enslaved in the United States today. A portion of these people are involved in sex trafficking, while sweatshops are the main place of business (Bales 2005, 93). In April 1998, the Smithsonian Institution took a daring step to address this issue and opened an exhibit titled, "Between a Rock and a Hard Place: A History of American Sweatshops, 1820–Present." The exhibit compared the history of labor with present realities. It introduced some of the important episodes of the history of sweatshops, and the exhibit explained the nature of sweatshops in a globalized economy. It served to expose how sweatshops and slavery exist, and even coexist, in the United States.

Many people in the American public were startled by this news, because they believed that the social reform and labor movements had eradicated the phenomenon of sweatshops. The centerpiece of the exhibit was a re-creation of the El Monte factory, where seventy-two Thai garment workers had recently worked in virtual slavery for brand-name clothing manufacturers and retailers. Some had worked for seven years behind razor wire and locked doors. The uncovering of this sweatshop became newsworthy in the United States (NMAH 1998).

In August 1995, federal and state police agents raided an apartment complex that was operating as an illegal sweatshop. Young women from Thai villages had been deceived into coming to the United States to work in sweatshops by ringleaders in their native land, recruited with the promise of a better life (Saunders 1999). However, when they arrived at the industrial compound, they were forced to work sixteen to eighteen hours a day for between $0.69 and $2.00 an hour. They were told that they would not be freed until they paid off their debt for their transportation to the United States. They also had to pay exorbitant prices for many of their necessities, including toiletries and food. These workers were under constant surveillance and physically and verbally abused, including threats of rape and murder. Their housing conditions were overcrowded and unsanitary, and they were confined to their quarters with doors locked from the outside (Louie 2001). Guards stood outside of their quarters, and a razor wire fence surrounded their compound (Bonacich and Appelbaum 2000; Liebhold and Rubenstein 2003; McGurrin 2007; Su 1997). The workers gained their freedom on 2 August 1995, but they were then imprisoned again for nine days while the Immigration and Naturalization Service (INS) deliberated on their future. In 1996, they were granted legal residency with the right to work in the United States (Liebhold and Rubenstein 2003, 59–60; Louie 2001). The conditions of exploitation and the threat of violence against these workers continue to be widespread throughout the globe (E. Brooks 2007, xviii). The Smithsonian exhibit faced opposition from clothing manufacturers, who tried to block its opening. This reaction led museums in San Francisco, Chicago, and New York to cancel the exhibit when it was scheduled to travel later that year (Liebhold and Rubenstein 2003, 70).

While much of the US textile industry has moved offshore and landed in East Asia and South Asia, some factories were attracted to US territories in the western Pacific. The Commonwealth of the Northern Mariana Islands is one of these places, where industry was centered in the city of Saipan. Neils Jensen, a Christian missionary from New Zealand who has lived intermittently in Saipan since 1983, noted, "It certainly has its parallels to slavery or indentured servitude." He said, "Many of these workers go into debt for what they think will be the privilege of working on Saipan. Because they're so deeply in debt, they can't afford to retaliate or complain or leave. Their conditions are horrendous" (quoted in Shenon 1993).

Apologists for sweatshops argue that the global apparel trade brings economic development to the poorest regions of the world with better employment and increased wages. However, because many factory owners compete for orders with low bids, the welfare of workers is often overlooked in the pursuit of low-cost production. It is the factory owner who dictates the terms of employment, and weak or no enforcement of local labor laws exacerbate the problem. Also, many of the current labor conditions and the growth of sweatshops force us to question whether wealth trickles down the economic ladder in developing countries (Rosen 2002, 5; R. Ross 2004).

This poor treatment of textile workers has re-emerged in the United States (Ellis and Tran 2016). While much of the textile industry has been exported to other regions of the world, there seems to be an increase in sweatshop violations in the United States. Consumers believe that buying clothing with the "Made in the USA" label means that they are purchasing products made under humane conditions. However, a 2015 survey of workers in the Los Angeles garment center found that "21 percent of workers have experienced physical or verbal violence on the job and 6 percent reported sexual harassment in the workplace. Half complained of poor ventilation, and eye and nose irritation from chemicals. A third of the workers surveyed reported a lack of clean drinking water at work and almost a third said they are not allowed to take rest breaks" (El Nasser 2015). They work overtime without compensation and earn an average of $5 an hour (El Nasser 2015; Little and Shackel 2014; Shackel 2018b).

With a very low standard of living, many countries like Bangladesh have attracted low-capital industries, like the ready-made garment industry. Since gaining its independence from Pakistan, Bangladesh has had three major coups and two dozen smaller rebellions. The country ranks 130 out of 139 countries for its roads, power, and ports, according to the World Economic Forum's Global Competitiveness Report (Srivastava 2013). Multinational retailers arrived in Bangladesh expecting low prices, which in turn made local producers cut costs in building maintenance, safety, and wages (Chakravartty and Luce 2013). Cost-cutting measures in maintenance and safety led to several workplace disasters, with the Rana Plaza tragedy attracting international attention in 2013 when over one thousand workers were killed and many thousands more injured in a building collapse. According to the World Bank, the per capita income in Bangladesh was about $64 a month in 2011, while the minimum wage for a garment worker was $38 a month. This wage nearly doubled in 2013 as a result of violent protests related to the Rana Plaza incident (Hossain 2013).

Marikana and Soma

Since places like northeastern Pennsylvania support the heritage of the mining industry and are working to remember one of its most fatal protests, the Lattimer massacre, it becomes easy to believe that these tragedies associated with poor working conditions and negligence of mine operators are part of our past. However, the incident in Marikana, South Africa, provides a glimpse into a resource-rich developing economy where workers are underpaid and work in dreadful conditions. They were fired upon when they protested for a living wage.

The incident at Soma is another example where corporations placed profit ahead of safety, which resulted in the fatal accident that killed over three hundred workers. A subsequent criminal investigation showed that the miners were working in dangerous conditions. Miners also described the ineffective inspections, the lack of implementing safety standards, and the lack of adequate safety equipment. The company ignored warnings of elevated firedamp levels and rising heat (Human Rights Watch 2015).

While it is easy for us to see these events as part of the American past or believe that these incidents have been offshored to other regions of the world, similar tragedies are still part of our US industry (Little and Shackel 2014). On 29 April 2010, miners died in a Massey Energy operation as a result of thousands of safety violations in recent years. The company faced a federal criminal investigation for neglect and reckless practices. When CEO Don Blankenship visited the National Press Club he complained about the "knee-jerk political reactions to the incident." He also called for the Obama administration to lighten the regulations on the coal industry. Blankenship explained, "Corporate business is what built

America, in my opinion, and we need to let it thrive by, in a sense, leaving it alone" (Milbank 2010, A17).

When Blankenship was asked what Massey could have done to prevent the explosion that killed the miners, he responded, "I probably should've sued MSHA (Mine Safety and Health Administration)." He stated that MSHA and the EPA were "impeding their ability to pursue their careers, or their happiness" (Milbank 2010, A17). He also minimized the accident by stating, "There's 42,000 people killed a year on the highways" (Milbank 2010, A17). Blankenship was found guilty of one misdemeanor charge of conspiring to willfully violate mine safety and health standards, and sentenced to one year in prison and fined $250,000. He was released on 10 May 2017 (Bruggers 2017). While the American justice system seems to move slowly, the final outcome of the Soma trials took four years, and the results of Marikana are still pending.

Remembering Class Heritage

This book is more than a historical account of labor's role in the past in a relatively small region in the United States. Rather, it is important to think about anthracite heritage as playing a historical role in the development of social and economic inequalities based on the racialization of groups of people, which influenced the social and work structures in a developing industrialist capitalist society. By connecting these issues of race, labor, and capitalism to the present, we can see how many of the injustices of the past continue to plague contemporary communities in the United States as well as in developing countries. When we see environmental destruction, decaying factory buildings, and abandoned domestic sites, it is easy to think about the past. When viewing these remnants of past industry, we need to determine how we can use the past in the present to help mobilize us and put into action our support for social justice issues. It is important to move out of our comfort zone and connect these decaying places, these remnants of historical issues of labor injustice, to the present, even when it becomes politically dangerous to do so as we confront the hidden realities of a global economy (Smith et al. 2011).

While the United States recently commemorated the sesquicentennial of the Civil War, there continues to be a war on labor, as workers see their rights and ability to bargain slowly disappearing. At the turn of twentieth century, anti-unionism developed as a reaction to immigrant radicalism, which was sometimes violent and seen as subversive to the government. After World War I the American Legion and other patriotic groups served as the anti-labor militants who broke picket lines and committed violence against union activities. The New Deal policies gave trade unions a form of legal and ethical legitimacy as a way to counter the concentrated power of corporations. From the end of World War II until the 1960s, business and unions coexisted. However, the 1947 Taft-Hartley Act allowed states to pass "right to work" laws, which undermined the bargaining power of unions (Lichtenstein 2011, B6–B7).

In the 1930s and 1940s unions did not succeed in the South, mostly because racial tensions hampered the building of working-class solidarity. A large gap in wages existed between the North and the South, and many northern industries relocated to the South. The passing of civil rights legislation made the South seem less foreign to northern capitalists (Meyerson 2011, A15).

Companies like Walmart, which was founded in 1962, are now America's leading private sector employers. Walmart is ferociously anti-union, and the company opposed President Kennedy's efforts to extend a minimum wage to cover retail workers. Walmart developed an economic model that needed low-wage workers who were compelled to shop at the lowest-priced store. As Walmart grew it needed lower-priced goods, which meant that many of the suppliers in the United States turned to China for cheap labor and low-cost goods. This model of enterprise moved north in tandem with Ronald Reagan's election. The movement of southern capital north and the hostility toward unions intensified and became the norm for American business. Low-wage jobs are plentiful while middle-wage jobs have decreased, and the nonunion labor system has prevailed. As a counter, some northern and western states have enacted living wage laws (Meyerson 2011, A15).

So, when we look at the past in northeastern Pennsylvania, or any other place in the United States, we have the power to confront contemporary inequalities. Examples from the past can be used to illuminate connections to current social, political, and economic issues. Many of the social injustices that existed in the United States over a hundred years ago still exist to some extent in the United States or have been exported to other parts of the world. Most large-scale corporations work to make labor inequity invisible, keeping workers and their concerns at the periphery of any discussion related to issues of social justice in the workplace.

While archaeology has traditionally focused on issues related to consumption, it is clear that consumption leads to destruction. González-Ruibal (2008, 261) explains that "the vegetarians eating soy in a European metropolis unwittingly foster the destruction of the Amazonian rain forest, while the consumption of diamonds in North America favors the dreadful mutilation of several thousand Liberians." By examining the destructive process, archaeology allows us to expose the structure and relations of power. And in the materials found in this book, it is the consumption of everyday twentieth and twenty-first century material culture that is connected to the destruction of the environment of northeastern Pennsylvania, the collapse of factory buildings in Bangladesh, the protests of miners in South Africa, mine disasters in Turkey, and the transgenerational impacts of noncontagious diseases found in US communities that faced environmental, labor, and nutritional trauma.

There is a connectedness, a type of genealogy, which links the past results of unchecked capitalism to the present. The mines and the factories that developed over a century ago in the Western Hemisphere are necessarily connected to the mines and factories half a globe away. While they are different corporations and separated by over a century of time, they are connected through the system of unchecked capitalism. The persistence of unchecked capitalism connects the meaning of these places. It is the poor, subaltern groups that lack the power to change this oppressive system. They are enveloped by the system, powerless.

By bringing to light the conditions of the past and connecting these issues to the present, we can make some of these difficult histories a platform from which to discuss the continued prevalence of these inequities. If we can change the memory of an event, we change what is important in the public memory, and we change the contemporary conversation as people work through what lessons they draw from the past. That is why the difficult labor histories and the memorialization at places in northeastern Pennsylvania, Savar Upazila of Dhaka District, Bangladesh, Marikana, South Africa, and Soma, Turkey, are important touchstones to learn and teach about inequalities and social justice issues related to work and labor. These are only a few places that we remember; unfortunately, there are many more that are not part of the public memory. By having difficult conversations about the past, we can advance our commitment to address inequality and social justice issues today.

REFERENCES

Agassiz, Louis. 1850. "The Diversity of Origin of the Human Races." *Christian Examiner* 99: 110–45.

Al Jazeera. 2012a. "S. Africa's Lonmin Miners Return to Work: Miners on Strike for More than Six Weeks Resume Work as Strikes Continue at Other Mines." 20 September. http://www.aljazeera.com/news/africa/2012/09/201291915482540917.html.

Al Jazeera. 2012b. "South African Police Halt Peaceful Protest: Police Forces Persuade Striking Miners to Disperse One Day After Raids and Violent Clashes at Marikana." 16 September. http://www.aljazeera.com/news/africa/2012/09/20129157270511419.html.

Al Jazeera. 2012c. "Strikers March at S Africa's Platinum Mine: At Least 1,000 Protest at Mine Where Police Shot and Killed 34 Miners, Demanding a Pay Rise in Renewed Demonstration." 5 September. http://www.aljazeera.com/video/africa/2012/09/20129584616278329.html.

Al Jazeera. 2013a. "Hope Dims for Bangladesh Survivors." 29 April. www.aljazeera.com/news/asia/2013/04/2013428141142643708.html.

Al Jazeera. 2013b. "Protests spread in Bangladesh Amid Arrests." 29 April. www.aljazeera.com/video/asia/2013/04/201342782714571732.html.

Al Jazeera. 2017. "Rana Plaza Owner Jailed for Three Years over Corruption." 30 August. https://www.aljazeera.com/news/2017/08/rana-plaza-owner-jailed-years-corruption-170829161742916.html

Alam, Julhas. 2013. "Bangladesh Factory Collapse: Murder Investigation Opens Against Owner as Death Toll Hits 645." *Toronto Star*, 6 May. https://www.thestar.com/news/world/2013/05/06/bangladesh_factory_collapse_murder_investigation_opens_against_owner_as_death_toll_hits_645.html.

Alam, Julhas, and Chris Blake. 2013. "Bangladesh Building Collapse: Fire Breaks Out in Factory Wreckage." *Huffington Post*, 29 April. www.huffingtonpost.com/2013/04/28/bangladesh-building-collapse-fire-factory_n_3174732.html.

Alam, Julhas, and Farid Hossain. 2013. "Bangladesh Collapse Search Over; Death Toll 1,127." Yahoo News, 13 May. https://www.yahoo.com/news/bangladesh-collapse-search-over-death-toll-1-127-122554495.html.

Allan, Theodore W. 1994. *The Invention of the White Race*. Vol. 1. London: Verso.

Allen, Garland E. 1983. "The Misuse of Biological Hierarchies: The American Eugenics Movement, 1900–1940." *History and Philosophy of the Life Sciences* 5(2):105–28.

Allen, Garland E. 1986. "The Eugenics Record Office at Cold Spring Harbor, 1910–1940: An Essay in Institutional History." *Osiris* 2: 225–64.

Arnold, Andrew B. 2014. *Fueling the Gilded Age: Railroads, Miners and Disorder in Pennsylvania Coal Country*. New York: New York University Press.

Badcock, Anna, and Robert Johnston. 2013. "Protest." In *The Oxford Handbook of the Archaeology of the Contemporary World*, ed. Graves-Brown, Paul, Rodney Harrison, and Angela Piccin, 321–35. Oxford: Oxford University Press.

BadCredit.org. 2015. "America's 20 Most Overindulgent Metropolitan Areas." http://www.badcredit.org/americas-20-overindulgent-metropolitan-areas.

Baker, Lee D., and Thomas C. Patterson. 1994. "Race, Racism, and the History of U.S. Anthropology." *Transforming Anthropology* 5(1–2):1–7.

Bales, Kevin. 2004. *Disposable People: New Slavery in the Global Economy*. Berkeley: University of California Press.

Bales, Kevin. 2005. *Understanding Global Slavery: A Reader*. Berkeley: University of California Press.

Barkan, Elazar. 1992. *The Retreat of Scientific Racism: Changing Concepts of Race in Britain and the United States between the World Wars*. Cambridge: Cambridge University Press.

Barker, D. 2002. "Fetal Programming of Coronary Heart Disease." *Trends in Endocrinology and Metabolism Trends in Endocrinology and Metabolism* 13(9): 364–68.

Barker, David, and Kent Thornburg. 2013. "The Obstetric Origins of Health for a Lifetime." *Clinical Obstetrics and Gynecology* 56(3): 511–19.

BBC News. 2012a. "Marikana Mine Killings: South African Police 'Planted Weapons.'" 6 November. http://www.bbc.com/news/world-africa-20218828.

BBC News. 2012b. "South Africa's Lonmin Marikana Mine Clashes Killed 34." 17 August. http://www.bbc.com/news/world-africa-19292909.

BBC News. 2012c. "South Africa's Marikana Mine Closed by 'Intimidation.'" 27 August. http://www.bbc.com/news/world-africa-19388584.

BBC News. 2014a. "Fury at Government over Worst Turkish Mine Disaster." 14 May. http://www.bbc.com/news/world-europe-27415813.

BBC News. 2014b. "Turkish Mine Disaster: PM Erdogan's Car Attacked." 14 May. http://www.bbc.com/news/world-europe-27415296.

BBC News. 2014c. "Turkish Mine Disaster: Unions Hold Protest Strike." 15 May.

Beik, Mildred Allen. 2002. "The Significance of the Lattimer Massacre: Who Owns Its History?" In "The Lattimer Massacre (1897)," special issue, *Pennsylvania History: A Journal of Mid-Atlantic Studies* 69(1): 58–70.

Bench Marks Foundation. 2012. "What Government Needs to Do to Prevent Another 'Marikana.'" 4 October. http://www.bench-marks.org.za/press/bench_marks_foundation_government_interventions.pdf.

Benedict, Ruth. 1940. *Race: Science and Politics*. New York: Modern Age Publishers.
Benjamin, W., and R. Tiedemann. 1999. *The Arcades Project*. Cambridge, MA: Belknap.
Berkes, Howard. 2014. "The Turkish Mine Disaster: How Could It Happen?" NPR, 15 May. http://www.npr.org/sections/thetwo-way/2014/05/15/312563946/the-turkish-mine-disaster-how-could-it-happen.
Berman, Marshall. 1982. *All that Is Solid Melts into Air: The Experience of Modernity*. New York: Penguin.
Blakey, Michael L. 1987. "Intrinsic Social and Political Bias in the History of American Physical Anthropology: With Special Reference to the Work of Aleš Hrdlička." *Critique of Anthropology* 7(2): 7–35. doi: 10.1177/0308275X8700700203.
Blaschak Coal Company. 2017. "The Anthracite Advantage: A Fact Sheet on Anthracite Coal." http://www.blaschakcoal.com/wp-content/uploads/Anthracite-Advantage-Fact-Sheet1.pdf.
Blatz, Perry K. 1994. *Democratic Miners: Work and Labor Relations in the Anthracite Coal Industry, 1875–1925*. Albany: State University of New York Press.
Blatz, Perry K. 2002. "Reflections on Lattimer: A Complex and Significant Event." In "The Lattimer Massacre (1897)," special issue, *Pennsylvania History: A Journal of Mid-Atlantic Studies* 69(1): 42–51.
Bluestone, Barry, and Bennett Harrison. 1982. *The Deindustrialization of America: Plant Closings, Community Abandonment, and the Dismantling of Basic Industry*. New York: Basic Books.
Boas, Franz. [1906] 1974. "Commencement Address for Atlanta University." In *A Franz Boas Reader*, ed. George W. Stocking Jr., 311–16. Chicago: University of Chicago Press.
Boas, Franz. 1910. "The Real Race Problem." *The Crisis* 1: 5.
Boas, Franz. 1911a. "The Instability of Human Types." In *Papers on Inter-Racial Problems Communicated to the First Universal Races Congress Held at the University of London, July 26–29, 1911*, ed. G. Spiller, 99–103. London: P. S. King and Son.
Boas, Franz. 1911b. *The Mind of the Primitive Man*. New York: Macmillan.
Boas, Franz. 1912. *Changes in Bodily Form of Descendants of Immigrants*. New York: Columbia University Press.
Boas, Franz. 1940. *Race, Language, and Culture*. New York: Macmillan.
Boas, Franz. 1945. *Race and Democratic Society*. New York: J. J. Augustin Publisher.
Bodnar, John E. 1982. *Immigration and Modernization: The Case of Slavic Peasants in Industrial America*. St. Paul, MN: Immigration History Research Center, University of Minnesota.
Bodnar, John. 1983. *Anthracite People: Families, Unions, and Work, 1900–1940*. Harrisburg: Pennsylvania Historical and Museum Commission.

Bohman, Dave. 2012. "Coal Region Ghost Towns." WNEP, 6 February. http://wnep.com/2011/08/10/coal-region-ghost-towns/oal.

Bonacich, Edna, and Richard P. Appelbaum. 2000. *Behind the Label: Inequality in the Los Angeles Apparel Industry*. Berkeley: University of California Press.

Brave Heart, Maria Yellow Horse. 1999. "Gender Differences in the Historical Trauma Response among the Lakota." *Journal of Health & Social Policy* 10(4): 1–21.

Brave Heart, Maria Yellow Horse. 2003. "The Historical Trauma Response among Natives and its Relationship with Substance Abuse: A Lakota Illustration." *Journal of Psychoactive Drugs* 35(1): 7.

Brinton, Daniel G. 1890a. *Essays of an Americanist*. Philadelphia: Porter and Coates.

Brinton, Daniel G. 1890b. *Races and Peoples: Lectures on the Science of Ethnography*. New York: N. D. C. Hodges.

Brooks, Ethel C. 2007. *Unraveling the Garment Industry: Transnational Organizing and Women's Work*. Minneapolis: University of Minnesota Press.

Brooks, John Graham. 1898. "Notes." *The Yale Review: A Quarterly Journal for the Scientific Discussion of Economic, Political and Social Questions* 6: 306–11.

Brown, Kate. 2015. *Dispatches from Dystopia: Histories of Places Not Yet Forgotten*. Chicago: University of Chicago Press.

Bruggers, James. 2017. "Former Coal Baron and Kentucky Native Don Blankenship Ready for Prison Release." *Courier-Journal*, 10 May. http://www.courier-journal.com/story/news/crime/2017/05/10/former-coal-baron-and-kentucky-native-don-blankenship-ready-prison-release/316299001.

Bump, Philip. 2012. "Black Lung Disease, Once on the Brink of Extinction, Is Back. Thank the Coal Industry." *Grist: A Beacon in the Smog*, 9 July. http://grist.org/news/black-lung-disease-once-on-the-brink-of-extinction-is-back-thank-the-coal-industry.

Burk, Jason. 2014. "Rana Plaza: One Year on from the Bangladesh Factory Disaster." *Guardian*, 19 April. https://www.theguardian.com/world/2014/apr/19/rana-plaza-bangladesh-one-year-on.

Butler, Sarah. 2013. "Bangladeshi Factory Deaths Spark Action Among High-Street Clothing Chains." *Guardian*, 20 July. https://www.theguardian.com/world/2013/jun/23/rana-plaza-factory-disaster-bangladesh-primark.

Bygren, Lars Olov, Petter Tinghög, John Carstensen, Soren Edvinsson, Gunnar Kaati, Marcus E. Pembrey, and Michael Sjöström. 2014. "Change in Paternal Grandmothers' Early Food Supply Influenced Cardiovascular Mortality of the Female Grandchildren." *BMC Genetics* 15(1): 12. doi: 10.1186/1471-2156-15-12.

Calamur, Krishnadev. 2013. "Deadly Bangladesh Collapse: Building Owner Arrested." Rhode Island Public Radio, 28 April. http://ripr.org/post/deadly-bangladesh-collapse-building-owner-arrested.

CDC (Centers for Disease Control and Prevention). 2015. "Statistically Significant Drug Overdose Death Rate Increase from 2014–2015." Atlanta: Centers for Disease Control and Prevention. https://www.cdc.gov/drugoverdose/data/statedeaths.html.

Chakravartty, Paula, and Stephanie Luce. 2013. "May Day: Reflecting on Bangladesh Factory Disaster and Corporate Terror; The Manifestation of the 'Race to the Bottom' Contributes Directly to Increasing Rates of Inequality in Bangladesh." *Al Jazeera*, 3 May. http://www.aljazeera.com/indepth/opinion/2013/05/201351104516268273.html.

Chase, Allan. 1980. *The Legacy of Malthus: The Social Costs of the New Scientific Racism*. Urbana: University of Illinois Press.

Clark, Krissy. 2013. "U.S. Retailers See Fallout from Bangladesh Factory Fire." Marketplace's Wealth & Poverty Desk, Marketplace, 29 April. https://www.marketplace.org/2012/11/28/world/us-retailers-see-fallout-bangladesh-factory-fire.

Coal Age. 1914. *Coal Age: Devoted to Coal Mining and Coal Manufacturing* 6(10).

Collier, Robert. 1999. "Saipan Workers Describe Slavery of Sweatshops / They Say American Dream Turned into Nightmare." SFGate, 22 January. http://www.sfgate.com/news/article/Saipan-Workers-Describe-Slavery-of-Sweatshops-2950970.php.

Conlogue, Bill. 2013. *Here and There: Reading Pennsylvania's Working Landscapes*. University Park: Penn State University Press.

Cornell, Robert J. 1957. *The Anthracite Coal Strike of 1902*. Washington DC: Catholic University Press.

Cowie, Jefferson, and Joseph Heathcott, eds. 2003. *Beyond the Ruins: The Meanings of Deindustrialization*. Ithaca, NY: Cornell University Press.

Craighill, Cassady. 2014. "What Caused the Turkey Coal Mine Disaster and How to Stop It From Ever Happening Again." Greenpeace, 20 May. http://www.greenpeace.org/usa/caused-turkey-coal-mine-disaster-stop-ever-happening.

Cruz Cuison, Rose. 2000. "The Construction of Labor Abuse in the Mariana Islands as Anti-American." *UCLA Asian Pacific American Law Journal* 6: 61–85.

D'Agostino, Peter. 2002. "Craniums, Criminals, and the 'Cursed Race': Italian Anthropology in American Racial Thought, 1861–1924." *Comparative Studies in Society and History* 44(2): 319–43. doi: https://doi.org/10.1017/S0010417502000154.

Daily Sabah. 2016. "Pain Lingers 2 Years after Soma Mining Disaster, Turkey's Deadliest." 13 May. https://www.dailysabah.com/turkey/2016/05/13/pain-lingers-2-years-after-soma-mining-disaster-turkeys-deadliest.

Davis, Rebecca. 2014. "Marikana, Two Years On: Cape Town's Protest Artists Remember the Dead." *Daily Maverick*, 15 August. https://www.dailymaverick.co.za/article/2014-08-15-marikana-two-years-on-cape-towns-protest-artists-remember-the-dead/#.wm7qsvkrliv.

Dawdy, Shannon Lee. 2010. "Clockpunk Anthropology and the Ruins of Modernity." *Current Anthropology* 51(6): 761–93.

Daxinger, L., and E. Whitelaw. 2012. "Understanding Transgenerational Epigenetic Inheritance via the Gametes in Mammals." *Nature Reviews Genetics* 13(3): 153–62. doi: 10.1038/nrg3188.

De Backer, Guy. 2008. "Risk Factors and Prevention of Cardiovascular Disease: A Review." *Dialogues* 13(2): 83–90.

de la Torre, Ferdie. 2007. "Dotts: It's the End for All CNMI Garment Factories." *Saipan Tribune*, 30 May. http://www.saipantribune.com/newsstory.aspx?cat=1&newsID=68959.

De León, Jason, 2012. "'Better to Be Hot than Caught': Excavating the Conflicting Roles of Migrant Material Culture." *American Anthropologist* 114(3): 477–95. doi: 10.1111/j.1548-1433.2012.01447.

De Waal, Mandy. 2012. "Marikana: NPA Drops 'Common Purpose' Charges, But Critical Questions Remain." *Daily Maverick* (South Africa), 3 September. https://www.dailymaverick.co.za/article/2012-09-03-marikana-npa-drops-common-purpose-charges-but-critical-questions-remain.

De Wet, P. 2012. "Marikana: How the Wage War was Won." *Mail and Guardian*, 21 September. http://Mg.co.za/article/2012-09-21-00-marikana-how-the-wage-war-was-won.

Deasy, George F., and Phyllis R. Griess. 1961. "Tourism for the Anthracite Region: An Alternative for Unemployment." *Mineral Industries* 30(7): 1–8.

Devakumar, Delan, Marion Birch, David Osrin, Egbert Sondorp, and Jonathan C. Wells. 2014. "The Intergenerational Effects of War on the Health of Children." *BMC Medicine* 12(1): 57.

Dewbury, Adam. 2007. "The American School and Scientific Racism in Early American Anthropology." *Histories of Anthropology Annual* 3: 121–47.

Dixon, James R. 2013. "Two Riots: The Importance of Civil Unrest in Contemporary Archaeology." In *The Oxford Handbook of the Archaeology of the Contemporary World*, ed. Graves-Brown, Paul, Rodney Harrison, and Angela Piccin, 351–63. Oxford: Oxford University Press.

Dublin, Thomas. 1998. *When the Mines Closed: Stories of Struggles in Hard Times*. Ithaca, NY: Cornell University Press.

Dublin, Thomas, and Walter Licht. 2005. *The Face of Decline: The Pennsylvania Anthracite Region in the Twentieth Century*. Ithaca, NY: Cornell University Press.

Dulles, Foster Rhea, and Melvyn Dubofsky. 1984. *Labor in America: A History*. 4th ed. Arlington Heights, IL: Harlan Davidson.

Earth Conservancy. 2017. "Anthracite Mining in Northeastern Pennsylvania." http://www.earthconservancy.org/projects/reclamation.

Economist. 2014. "Turkey's Mining Disaster: Grim News Underground." 14 May. http://www.economist.com/blogs/charlemagne/2014/05/turkeys-mining-disaster.

Editorial Board. 2016. "Don't Let Coal Decline Stop Reclamation." *Times Tribune* (Scranton, PA), 18 January. http://thetimes-tribune.com/opinion/don-t-let-coal-decline-stop-reclamation-1.1996551#.Vp0JC3dooJ8.facebook.

Ellis, Kristi, and Khanh T. L. Tran. 2016. "Sweatshops Persist in U.S. Garment Industry: Sweatshop Conditions Are Still Found in Garment Factories in California 20 Years After Investigators Uncovered One of the Most Egregious Examples in El Monte, Calif." 5 December. http://wwd.com/business-news/government-trade/sweatshops-persist-in-u-s-garment-industry-10716742.

El Nasser, Haya. 2015. "LA Garment Industry Rife with Sweatshop Conditions: New Study Reveals Almost Half the Garment Workers Labor 10 Hours or More a Day without Overtime Pay." *Al Jazeera America*, 9 September. http://america.aljazeera.com/articles/2015/9/9/sweatshop-conditions-in-la-garment-industry.html.

Erimtan, Can. 2014. "The Soma Mine Disaster or Privatization Gone Wild in Turkey." RT, 16 May. https://www.rt.com/op-edge/159420-erdogan-turkey-mine-disaster.

Evans-Campbell, T. 2008. "Historical Trauma in American Indian/Native Alaska Communities: A Multilevel Framework for Exploring Impacts on Individuals, Families, and Communities." *Journal of Interpersonal Violence* 23(3): 316–38. doi: 10.1177/0886260507312290.

Ewall, Mike. 2017. "Waste Coal." *Energy Justice Network*. http://www.energyjustice.net/coal/wastecoal.

Farmer, Paul. 1996. "On Suffering and Structural Violence: A View from Below." *Daedalus* 125(1): 261–283.

Farmer, Paul. 2004. "An Anthropology of Structural Violence." *Current Anthropology* 45(3): 305–25.

Fink, Leon. 2015. *The Long Gilded Age: American Capitalism and the Lessons of a New World Order*. Philadelphia: University of Pennsylvania Press.

First Catholic Slovak Ladies Union. 1952. *The Anniversary Slovak-American Cook Book*. Chicago: Tylka Brothers Press.

Fletcher, Pascal. 2012. "South Africa's 'Hill of Horror': Self-Defense or Massacre? Protesting Miners React as the Police Shot at Them Outside a South African Mine in Rustenburg, 100 Km (62 Miles) Northwest of Johannesburg." Reuters, 17 August. http://www.reuters.com/article/us-safrica-lonmin-shooting-idusbre87g0ms20120817.

Fogel, Benjamin. 2013. "Marikina: 1 Year Later." *Amandla: South Africa's New Progressive Magazine Standing for Social Justice*, 23 February. http://www.amandla.org.za/amandla-magazine/current-issue/1793-marikana-1-year-later--by-benjamin-fogel.

Foner, Philip S. 1964. *History of the Labor Movement in the United States*. Vol 3. New York: International Publishers.

Fowles, Severin. 2010. "Response to 'Clockpunk Anthropology and the Ruins of Modernity.'" *Current Anthropology* 51(6): 780–81.

Futterman, L. G., and L. Lemberg. 1998. "Fifty Percent of Patients with Coronary Artery Disease Do Not Have Any of the Conventional Risk Factors." *American Journal of Critical Care* 7(3): 240–44.

Gallo, Alexandra. 2017. "More Holes Open on Property of Family Who Nearly Lost Home." WNEP, 30 January. http://wnep.com/2017/01/30/more-holes-open-on-property-of-family-who-nearly-lost-home.

Gallup-Heathways. 2014. "Well Being Index." *State of American Well-Being: 2013 State, Community, and Congressional District Analysis.* Gallup-Healthways Well-Being Index. http://www.well-beingindex.com.

Galski, Sam. 2012. "Hazle Residents Ask for Help with Quarry Dust, Noise Issues." *Standard Speaker*, 10 July, A5. http://standardspeaker.com/news/hazle-residents-ask-for-help-with-quarry-dust-noise-issues-1.1341259.

Galtung, Johan. 1969. "Violence, Peace, and Peace Research." *Journal of Peace Research* 6(3): 167–91.

Galtung, Johan. 1990. "Cultural Violence." *Journal of Peace Research* 27(3): 291–305.

Guardian. 2014. "Turkish PM's Aide Given Sick Leave after Kicking Mine Disaster Protester." 19 May. https://www.theguardian.com/world/2014/may/19/turkish-pm-aide-sick-leave-kicking-mine-disaster-protester.

Guardian. 2015. "Unrest as Turkey Begins Soma Mine Disaster Trial: Dozens of Managers and Employees Have Gone on Trial over Turkey's Worst Mining Disaster, Which Left 301 Coalminers Dead." 13 April. https://www.theguardian.com/world/2015/apr/13/unrest-as-turkey-begins-soma-mine-disaster-trial.

Glaeser, Edward L., Joshua D. Gottlieb, and Oren Ziv. 2014. "Unhappy Cities." Working Paper 20291, National Bureau of Economic Research. http://www.nber.org/papers/w2029.

Glazer, Nathan, and Daniel P. Moynihan. 1963. *Beyond the Melting Pot*. Cambridge, MA: MIT Press.

Gluckman, Peter, Mark Hanson, Cyrus Cooper, and Kent L. Thornburg. 2008. "Effect of In Utero and Early-Life Conditions on Adult Health and Disease." *New England Journal of Medicine* 359(1): 61–73.

Goin, Peter, and Elizabeth Raymond. 2001. "Living in Anthracite: Mining Landscape and Sense of Place in Wyoming Valley, Pennsylvania." *The Public Historian* 23(2): 29–45.

Goin, Peter, and C. Elizabeth Raymond. 2004. *Changing Mines in America*. Santa Fe, NM, and Staunton, VA: Center for American Places.

González-Ruibal, Alfredo. 2008. "Time to Destroy: An Archaeology of Supermodernity." *Current Anthropology* 49(2): 247–79.

Gordillo, Gaston R. 2014. *Rubble: The Afterlife of Destruction*. Durham, NC: Duke University Press.

Gossett, Thomas F. 1963. *Race: The History of an Idea in America*. Dallas: Southern Methodist University Press.

Graham, G. 2014. "Population-Based Approaches to Understanding Disparities in Cardiovascular Disease Risk in the United States." *International Journal of General Medicine* 7: 393–400.
Greene, Victor R. 1968. *The Slavic Community on Strike: Immigrant Labor in Pennsylvania Anthracite.* Notre Dame, IN: University of Notre Dame Press.
Griess, Phyllis R., and George F. Deasy. 1964. "Economic Impact of a Pennsylvania Tourist Facility." *Land Economics* 40(2): 213–220.
Guglielmo, Thomas. 1999. "Toward Essentialism, Toward Difference: Gino Speranza and Conceptions of Race and Italian-American Racial Identity, 1900–1925." *Mid-America: An Historical Review* 81(2): 169–213.
Halpin, James. 2014. "Region's Residents among Most Miserable." *Citizen's Voice*, 7 April. http://citizensvoice.com/news/region-s-residents-among-most-miserable-1.1663700.
Hambidge, Jay. 1898. "An Artist's Impression of the Colliery Region." *The Century* 55(6): 822–27. Available at http://digital.library.cornel.edu.
Handlin, Oscar. 1950. *Race and Nationality in American Life.* Garden City, NY: Doubleday Anchor.
Handlin, Oscar. 1957. *Race and Nationality in American Life.* Boston, MA: Little, Brown.
Haraway, Donna J. 1989. *Primate Visions: Gender, Race, and Nature in the World of Modern Science.* New York: Routledge.
Harrison, Faye V. 1998. "Introduction: Expanding the Discourse on 'Race.'" *American Anthropologist* 100(3): 609–31.
Harrison, Rodney, and John Schofield. 2010. *After Modernity: Archaeological Approaches to the Contemporary Past.* Oxford: Oxford University Press.
Hastrup, Kristen, and Peter Elsass. 1990. "Anthropology Advocacy: A Contradiction in Terms?" *Current Anthropology* 31(3): 301–11.
Heron, Melonie. 2010. "Deaths: Leading Causes for 2010. N. V. S. Reports." *National Vital Statistics Reports* 62(6): 1–96.
High, Steven. 2013a. "Beyond Aesthetics: Visibility and Invisibility in the Aftermath of Deindustrialization." *International Labor and Working-Class History* 84: 140–53.
High, Steven. 2013b. "'The Wounds of Class': A Historiographical Reflection on the Study of Deindustrialization, 1973–2013." *History Compass* 11(11): 994–1007.
Hlongwane, Sipho. 2012. "Marikana: Freed Miners Speak of Torture in Police Cells." *Daily Maverick*, 4 September. https://www.dailymaverick.co.za/article/2012-09-04-marikana-freed-miners-speak-of-torture-in-police-cells#.WM7n7PkrLIV.
Holt, Sharon Ann. 2001. "The Life and Labour of Coxe Miners." *Pennsylvania Legacies* 1(1): 6–13.
Horsman, Reginald. 1981. *Race and Manifest Destiny: The Origins of American Racial Anglo-Saxonism.* Cambridge, MA: Harvard University Press.

Hossain, Farid. 2013. "Bangladesh Building-Collapse Death Toll Tops 600." *Washington Post*, 5 May. https://www.washingtonpost.com/world/asia_pacific/bangladesh-building-collapse-death-toll-tops-600/2013/05/05/2b5e071e-b5ad-11e2-92f3-f291801936b8_story.html?utm_term=.b55c536655e3.

Human Rights Watch. 2015. "Turkey: Mine Disaster Trial to Open. Company Officials Charged, But Government Failures Need Investigation." 13 April. https://www.hrw.org/news/2015/04/13/turkey-mine-disaster-trial-open.

Huyssen, Andreas. 2010. "Authentic Ruins: Products of Modernity." In *Ruins of Modernity*, ed. Julia Hell and Andreas Schonle, 17–28. Durham, NC: Duke University Press.

iAfrica.com. 2012. "Wage Deal Ends Marikana Strike." 20 September. http://news.iafrica.com/sa/817203.html.

ILO (International Labor Organization). 2012. "South Africa Could Do More for Miners, Says ILO Mining Specialist: The Killings of More than 30 Workers in the Marikana Platinum Mine Have Put the Spotlight on Working Conditions in South Africa's Mining Industry." 24 August. http://www.ilo.org/global/about-the-ilo/newsroom/news/WCMS_187783/lang--en/index.htm.

Jacobson, Matthew Frye. 1998. *Whiteness of a Different Color: European Immigrants and the Alchemy of Race*. Cambridge, MA: Harvard University Press.

Jacobson, Matthew Frye. 2001. *Barbarian Virtues: The United States Encounters Foreign Peoples at Home and Abroad, 1876–1917*. New York: Hill & Wang.

Jones, Eliot. 1914. *The Anthracite Coal Combination in the United States: With Some Account of the Early Development of the Anthracite Industry*. Cambridge, MA: Harvard University Press.

Keil, Thomas, and Jacqueline M. Keil. 2015. *Anthracite's Demise and the Post-Coal Economy of Northeastern Pennsylvania*. Bethlehem, PA: Lehigh University Press.

Kellor, Frances A. 1900. "Criminal Sociology: The American vs. the Latin School." *The Arena* 23(3): 301–4.

Kotsev, Victor. 2014. "Turkey Has One of World's Worst Mining Safety Records, and Experts Say Privatization Is Part of The Problem." *International Business Times*, 16 May. http://www.ibtimes.com/turkey-has-one-worlds-worst-mining-safety-records-experts-say-privatization-part-1585775.

Kuzawa, Christopher, and Elizabeth Sweet. 2009. "Epigenetics and the Embodiment of Race: Developmental Origins of US Racial Disparities in Cardiovascular Health." *American Journal of Human Biology* 21(1): 2–15.

Labowitz, Sarah, and Dorothée Baumann-Pauly. 2014. "Business as Usual Is Not an Option: Supply Chains & Sourcing after Rana Plaza." New York University Stern Center for Business and Human Rights, April. http://www.stern.nyu.edu/sites/default/files/assets/documents/con_047408.pdf.

Laing, A. 2012. "Striking South African Miners 'Were Shot in the Back.'" *Telegraph*, 27 August. http://www.telegraph.co.uk/news/worldnews/africaandindianocean/southafrica/9501910/Striking-South-African-miners-were-shot-in-the-back.html.

REFERENCES

Lam, Tong. 2013. *Abandoned Futures: A Journey to the Posthuman World*. London: Carpet Bombing Culture.

Lamparski, Nina, Patrick Jackson, Alison Daye, John Harrison, Jasmine Coleman, and Stephen Fottrell. 2014. "As It Happened: Turkey Mine Disaster." BBC News, 14 May. http://www.bbc.com/news/world-europe-27406195.

Langer, William L. 1975. "American Foods and Europe's Population Growth 1750–1850." *Journal of Social History*, 8(2): 51–66.

Learn, Jennifer. 1994. "Sewage Problems Plague County for Lack of Treatment Connections, Raw Sewage Has Been Ending Up in Creeks and Streams, and Many Communities Still Lag Behind in Making Changes." *Times Leader* (Scranton, PA), 19 June, 1A. http://archives.timesleader.com/1994_8/1994_06_19_SEWAGE_PROBLEMS_PLAGUE_COUNTY_FOR_LACK_OF_TREATMENT_CONNECTIONS_.html.

Letsch, Constanze. 2014. "Turkey: Miners and Mourners Scorn Government that 'Laughs at Our Pain': As Coalmine Disaster Death Toll Climbs Closer to 300, Mood in Suffering Town of Soma Oscillates between Devastation and Fury." *Guardian*, 15 May. https://www.theguardian.com/world/2014/may/15/mining-disaster-mourning-in-turkey.

Lichtenstein, Nelson. 2011. "The Long History of Labor Bashing." *Chronicle Review*, 11 March, B6–B7.

Liebhold, Peter, and Harry R. Rubenstein. 2003. "Bringing Sweatshops into the Museum." In *Sweatshop USA: The American Sweatshop in Historical and Global Perspective*, ed. Daniel Bender and Richard Greenwald, 57–73. New York: Routledge.

Liss, Julia. 1998. "Diasporic Identities: The Science and Politics of Race in the Work of Franz Boaz and W E.B. Du Bois, 1894–1919." *Cultural Anthropology* 13(2): 127–66.

Little, Barbara J., and Paul A. Shackel. 2014. *Archaeology, Heritage and Civic Engagement: Working Toward the Public Good*. Walnut Creek, CA: Left Coast Press.

Longazel, Jamie. 2016. *Undocumented Fears: Immigration and the Politics of Divide and Conquer in Hazleton, Pennsylvania*. Philadelphia: Temple University Press.

Louie, Miriam Ching Yoon. 2001. *Sweatshop Warriors: Immigrant Women Workers Take On the Global Factory*. Cambridge, MA: South End Press.

Lowen, Mark. 2015. "Turkey Mine Disaster: Raw Anger in Soma A Year On." BBC News, 13 May. http://www.bbc.com/news/world-europe-32709431.

Lowenthal, David. 1985. *The Past Is a Foreign Country*. Cambridge: Cambridge University Press.

Lucas, Gavin. 2013. "Ruins." In *The Oxford Handbook of the Archaeology of the Contemporary World*, ed. Graves-Brown, Paul, Rodney Harrison, and Angela Piccin, 192–203. Oxford: Oxford University Press.

Luconi, Stefano. 2016. "Black Dagoes? Italian Immigrants' Racial Status in the United States: An Ecological View." *Journal of Transatlantic Studies* 14(2): 188–99. doi: 10.1080/14794012.2016.1169869.

Lumey, L. H. 1992. "Decreased Birthweights in Infants after Maternal In Utero Exposure to the Dutch Famine of 1944–1945." Pediatric and Perinatal Epidemiology 6: 240–53.

MacGaffey, Janet. 2013. *Coal Dust on Your Feet: The Rise, Decline, and Restoration of an Anthracite Mining Town*. Lewisburg, PA: Bucknell University Press.

Mah, Alice. 2009. "Devastation but Also Home: Place Attachment in Areas of Industrial Decline." *Home Cultures* 6(3): 287–310.

Mah, Alice. 2010. "Memory, Uncertainty and Industrial Ruination: Walker Riverside, Newcastle upon Tyne." *International Journals of Urban and Regional Research* 34(2): 398–413.

Mah, Alice. 2012. *Industrial Ruination, Community and Place: Landscapes and Legacies of Urban Decline*. Toronto: University of Toronto Press.

Mailer, Tom. 2000. "Miners: Anthracite Coal Bosses Destroy the Environment." *The Militant* 64(37). http://www.themilitant.com/2000/6437/643752.html.

Marinovich, Greg. 2012. "The Murder Fields of Marikana. The Cold Murder Fields of Marikana." *Daily Maverick* (South Africa), 12 September. http://www.dailymaverick.co.za/article/2012-08-30-the-murder-fields-of-marikana-the-cold-murder-fields-of-marikana#.UUimOjckRFs.

Marsh, Ben. 1987. "Continuity and Decline in the Anthracite Towns of Pennsylvania." *Annals of the Association of Geographers* 77(3): 337–52.

McClenaghan, Maeve. 2012. "South African Massacre Was the Tip of an Iceberg." *The Bureau of Investigative Journalism*, 18 October. https://www.thebureauinvestigates.com/opinion/2012-10-18/south-african-massacre-was-the-tip-of-an-iceberg.

McEniry, Mary, and Alberto Palloni. 2010. "Early Life Exposures and the Occurrence and Timing of Heart Disease among the Older Adult Puerto Rican Population." *Demography* 47(1): 23–43.

McGlynn, Charles. 1992. "Great Debt Owed to Martyrs of Lattimer." *Standard Speaker* (Hazelton, PA), 2 September. News clipping on file, Luzerne County Historical Society, Wilkes-Barre, PA.

McGuire, Randall. 2008. *Archaeology as Political Action*. Berkeley: University of California Press.

McGurrin, Danielle. 2007. *Fabrication: Corporate and Governmental Crime in the Apparel Industry*. PhD dissertation. Tampa, FL: University of South Florida.

McHale, Margaret. 1913. *The C.W.C. Cook Book*. Scranton, PA: Catholic Women's Club.

Mendinsky, Justin J., and Brian A. Dempsey. 2004. "Effects of AMD Pollutant Loading on Streams in the Hazleton PA Area." National Meeting of the American Society of Mining and Reclamation, 18–24 April 2004, Morgantown, WV. Lexington, KY: ASMR. http://www.asmr.us/Portals/0/Documents/Conference-Proceedings/2004/1289-Mendinsky.pdf.

Metropolitan Area Situation & Outlook Report. 2016. Scranton–Wilkes-Barre–Hazleton, PA, Metropolitan Statistical Area. http://proximityone.com/metros/2013/cbsa42540.htm#1.

Meyerson, Harold. 2011. "An Ongoing Civil War." *Washington Post*, 13 April, A15.

Michaels, Cari, Rudy Rousseau, and Youa Yang. 2010. "Historical Trauma and Microaggressions: A Framework for Culturally-Based Practice." *Children's Mental Health eReview*, October, 1–9.

Milbank, Dana. 2010. "29 Dead, and a Coal CEO Blames Government." *Washington Post*, 25 July, A17.

Miller, Donald L., and Richard E. Sharpless. 1981. "The Ecological and Economic Impact of Anthracite Mining in Pennsylvania." In *Energy, Environment, and the Economy*, ed. Shyamal K. Majumdar, 169–83. Easton: Pennsylvania Academy of Science.

Miller, Donald L., and Richard E. Sharpless. 1998. *The Kingdom of Coal: Work, Enterprise, and Ethnic Communities in the Mine Fields*. Philadelphia: University of Pennsylvania Press.

Mims, Sekou, Larry Higginbottom, and Omar Reid. 2001. *Post Traumatic Slavery Disorder*. Dorchester, MA: Pyramid Builders.

Misulich, Robert J. 2011. "A Lesser-Known Immigration Crisis: Federal Immigration Law in the Commonwealth of the Northern Mariana Islands." *Pacific Rim Law & Policy Journal* 20(1): 211–35.

Mohatt, Nathaniel, and Jacob Tebes. 2014. "Historical Trauma as Public Narrative: A Conceptual Review of How History Impacts Present-Day Health." *Social Science & Medicine* 106: 128–36. doi: 10.1016/j.socscimed.20 14.01.043.

Montagu, Ashley. 1942. *Man's Most Dangerous Myth: The Fallacy of Race*. New York: Columbia University Press.

Morgan, Lewis Henry. 1877. *Ancient Society: Researches in the Line of Human Progress from Savagery through Barbarism to Civilization*. New York: Henry Holt.

Morton, Samuel George. 1839. *Crania Americana, or a Comparative View of the Skulls of Various Aboriginal Nations of North and South America*. Philadelphia: John Pennington.

Moyers, Bill, and Michael Winship. 2012. "GOP Defends Marianas' Sweatshops." Consortium News, 1 September. https://consortiumnews.com/2012/09/01/gop-defends-marianas-sweatshop.

Moynihan, Daniel P. 1965. "The Negro Family: The Case for National Action." Washington DC: US Department of Labor, Office of Policy Planning and Research.

Mukhopadhyay, Carol C., and Yolanda T. Moses. 1997. "Reestablishing 'Race' in Anthropological Discourse." *American Anthropologist* 99(3): 517–33.

New York Times. 1869a. "The Sunken Coal Mine: The Latest Pennsylvania Mining Horror—A Block of Houses Sink into a Mine—Ten Persons Engulfed—Apprehension of Further Disaster." 20 December.

New York Times. 1869b. "Ten or More Persons Buried Alive. Disaster in the Coal Region. Caving Is of a Pennsylvania Coal Mine. The Shaft Choked Up. Fall of Two Dwellings with the Bank." 19 December.

New York Times. 1924. "Veteran Buried by Mine Cave." 30 May.
Niceforo, Alfredo. 1898. *L'Italia Barbara Contemporanea* [Contemporary barbarian Italy]. Milano-Palermo: Remo Sandron.
Niceforo, Alfredo. 1901. *Italiani del Nord e Italiani del Sud* [Italians of the north and Italians of the south]. Turin: Fratelli Bocca.
Nielson, Robert. 2012. "Marikana Mine Massacre." *Whistling in the Wind*, 5 September. https://whistlinginthewind.org/2012/09/05/marikana-mine-massacre.
NMAH (National Museum of American History). 1998. *Between a Rock and a Hard Place: A History of American Sweatshops, 1820–Present*. Washington DC: National Museum of American History, Smithsonian Institution. http://www.americanhistory.si.edu/sweatshops.
Novak, Michael. 1978. *The Guns of Lattimer*. New York: Basic Books.
O'Bannon, Patrick, Marin Abbot, Susan Nabors, and James Parkinson. 1997. "Anthracite Industry in Northeastern, Pennsylvania, 1769–1945." National Register of Historic Places Multiple Property Documentation Form. Philadelphia, PA: Kise, Frank & Straw.
Omi, Michael, and Howard Winant. 1983. "By the River of Babylon: Race in the United States." *Socialist Review* 13: 31–65.
Orser, Charles E. 2001. *Race and the Archaeology of Identity*. Salt Lake City: University of Utah Press.
Orser, Charles E. 2007. *The Archaeology of Race and Racialization in Historic America*. Gainesville: University Press of Florida.
Our Lady of Grace Church. 2009. *Our Lady of Grace Church: 100th Anniversary, 1909–2009*. Hazleton, PA. Self-published.
Palladino, Grace. 2006. *Another Civil War: Labor, Capital, and the State in the Anthracite Regions of Pennsylvania, 1840–1868*. New York: Fordham University Press.
Patterson, Thomas C., and Frank Spencer. 1994. "Racial Hierarchies and Buffer Races." *Transforming Anthropology* 5(1–2): 20–27.
Pavalko, Ronald M. 1980. "Racism and the New Immigration: A Reinterpretation of the Assimilation of White Ethnics in American Society." *Sociology* 65(1): 56–77.
Pembrey, Marcus, Richard Saffery, Lars Olov Bygren, John Carstensen, Sören Edvinsson, Tomas Faresjö, Paul Franks, et al. 2014. "Human Transgenerational Responses to Early-Life Experience: Potential Impact on Development, Health and Biomedical Research." *Journal of Medical Genetics* 51(9): 563–72. doi: 10.1136/jmedgenet-2014-102577.
Phipps, R. M., and S. Degges-White. 2014. "A New Look at Transgenerational Trauma Transmission: Second-Generation Latino Immigrant Youth." *Journal of Multicultural Counseling and Development* 42(3): 174–87. doi: 10.1002/j.2161-1912.2014.00053.
Pick, Daniel. 1989. *Faces of Degeneration: A European Disorder, c.1848–c.1918*. Cambridge: Cambridge University Press.

Pinkowski, Edward. 1950. *Lattimer Massacre*. Philadelphia: Sunshine Press.

Powell, Benjamin H. 1980. "The Pennsylvania Anthracite Industry, 1769–1976." *Pennsylvania History* 47(1): 3–27. https://journals.psu.edu/phj/article/view/24141/23910.

Pulido, Laura. 1996. "A Critical Review of the Methodology of Environmental Racism Research." *Antipode* 28(2): 142–59.

Pullella, Philip. 2013. "Pope Condemns Bangladesh Working Conditions as 'Slave Labor.'" Reuters, 1 May. http://www.reuters.com/article/us-bangladesh-building-pope-idUSBRE9400VT20130501.

Quadir, Serajul. 2013. "Huge Bangladesh Fire Destroys Key Garments Factory." Reuters, 29 November. http://www.reuters.com/article/us-bangladesh-garments-fire-idUSBRE9AS05I20131129.

Rabinow, Paul. 1992. "For Hire: Resolutely Late Modern." In *Recapturing Anthropology*, ed. Richard Fox, 59–72. Santa Fe, NM: School of American Research Press.

Radosavljevich, Paul R. 1923. "Eugenic Problems of the Slavic Race." In *Second International Congress of Eugenics Held at the American Museum of Natural History, New York, September 22–28, 1921*, 154–65. Baltimore, MD: Williams and Wilkins.

Ragan, Tom. 2011. "Sewer Hookup Mandate Angers Tamaqua Residents." *Standard Speaker* (Hazleton, PA), 23 July. http://standardspeaker.com/news/sewer-hookup-mandate-angers-tamaqua-residents-1.1179172.

Ranker, Luke. 2015. "Scranton/W-B among Most Indulgent Cities." *Citizens Voice*, 17 March. http://citizensvoice.com/news/scranton-w-b-among-most-indulgent-cities-1.1849010.

Reynolds, Robert L. 1960. "The Coal Kings Come to Judgment." *American Heritage* 11(3). http://www.americanheritage.com/content/coal-kings-come-judgment.

Richards, John Stuart. 2002. *Early Coal Mining in the Anthracite Region*. Charleston, SC: Acadia Publishing.

Roberts, Kenneth L. 1922. *Why Europe Leaves Home*. Indianapolis: Bobbs-Merrill.

Roberts, Peter. 1901. *The Anthracite Coal Industry: A Study of Economic Conditions and Relations of the Cooperative Forces in the Development of the Anthracite Coal Industry of Pennsylvania*. New York: Macmillan.

Roberts, Peter. [1904] 1970. *Anthracite Coal Communities: A Study of the Demography, the Social, Educational and Moral Life of the Anthracite Regions*. New York: Arno Press and the New York Times.

Roberts, Peter. 1912. *The New Immigration*. New York: Macmillian.

Roediger, David R. 2005. *Working Toward Whiteness: How America's Immigrants Became White; The Strange Journey from Ellis Island to the Suburbs*. New York: Basic Books.

Roediger, David. 2007. *The Wages of Whiteness: Race and the Making of the American Working Class*. New York: Verso.

Roller, Michael P. 2015. "Migration, Modernity and Memory: The Archaeology of the Twentieth Century in a Northeast Pennsylvania Coal Company Town, 1897–2014." PhD dissertation. College Park, MD: Department of Anthropology, University of Maryland.

Roller, Michael P. 2018a. *An Archaeology of Structural Violence: Life in a Twentieth-Century Coal Town.* Gainesville: University of Florida Press.

Roller, Michael P. 2018b. "Late Modernity and Community Change in Lattimer No. 2: The American Twentieth Century as Seen through the Archaeology of a Pennsylvania Anthracite Town." *Historical Archaeology* 52: 70–84. doi.org/10.1007/s41636-017-0087-2.

Rood, Henry Edward. 1898. "A Pennsylvania Colliery Village: A Polyglot Community." *The Century* 55(6): 809–21. Available at http://digital.library.cornell.edu.

Roseberry, William. 1992. "Multiculturalism and the Challenge of Anthropology." *Social Research* 59(4): 841–58.

Rosen, Ellen Israel. 2002. *Making Sweatshops: The Globalization of the U.S. Apparel Industry.* Berkeley: University of California Press.

Ross, Edward Alsworth. 1914. "Italians in America." *The Century* 88 (July): 440.

Ross, Robert J. R. 2004. *Slaves to Fashion: Poverty and Abuse in the New Sweatshops.* Ann Arbor: University of Michigan Press.

Roucek, Joseph S. 1969. "The Image of the Slav in U.S. History and in Immigration Policy." *American Journal of Economics and Sociology* 28 (1): 29–48.

Roucek, Joseph S. 1976. "Neglected Aspects of the Slavs in American Historiography." *Ukrainian Quarterly* 32(1): 58–71.

Rowland, Jonathan. 2015. "Coal Dust Not a Danger to Luzerne Residents." *World Coal*, 19 November. https://www.worldcoal.com/mining/19112015/coal-dust-not-a-danger-to-luzerne-county-residents-blaschak-coal-3183.

Sacks, Karen B. 1989. "Toward a Unified Theory of Class, Race, and Gender." *American Ethnologist* 16(3): 534–550.

(SAPA) South African Press Association. 2012a. "Conflicting Accounts of Lonmin Shooting." *Independent Online*, 17 August. http://www.webcitation.org/6A0meTkoB.

(SAPA) South African Press Association. 2012b. "Lonmin, an Example of Exploitation." *Business Report*, 17 August. http://www.iol.co.za/business/companies/lonmin-an-example-of-exploitation-1.1365221#.UUiV4jckRFu.

(SAPA) South African Press Association. 2012c. "Marikana Inquiry Updates: 23 October." *Sapa Times*, 23 October. http://www.timeslive.co.za/local/2012/10/23/Marikana-inquiry-updates-23-October-2012.

Saunders. 1999. "Sweatshops Aren't History: Museum Traces Resurgence of Sweatshops in Exhibit Apparel Industry Tried to Stop." *New York Teacher*. www.newyorkteacher.org.

Scheper-Hughes, Nancy. 1995. "The Primacy of the Ethical: Propositions for a Militant Anthropology." *Current Anthropology* 36(3): 409–40.

Schumpeter, Joseph Alois. 1950. *Capitalism, Socialism, and Democracy*. New York: Harper.
Serres, Michel. 2000. *Retour au contrat naturel*. Paris: Bibliotheque National de France.
Shackel, Paul A. 2009. *The Archaeology of American Labor and Working-Class Life*. Gainesville: University Press of Florida.
Shackel, Paul A. 2013. "Reversing the Narrative: Using Archaeology to Challenge the Present and Change the Future." *Historical Archaeology* 47(3): 1–11.
Shackel, Paul A. 2016. "The Meaning of Place in the Anthracite Region of Northeastern Pennsylvania." *International Journal of Heritage Studies* 22 (3): 200–13. doi: 10.1080/13527258.2015.1114009.
Shackel, Paul A. 2017. "Anthracite Heritage: Landscape, Memory and the Environment." *Open Rivers: Rethinking Water, Place and Community*, no. 7 (Summer). http://editions.lib.umn.edu/openrivers/article/anthracite-heritage-landscape-memory-and-the-environment.
Shackel, Paul A. 2018a. *Remembering Lattimer: Migration, Labor, and Race in Pennsylvania Anthracite Country*. Champaign: University of Illinois Press.
Shackel, Paul A. 2018b. "Structural Violence and the Industrial Landscape." *International Journal of Heritage Studies* 25(7): 750–62. https://doi.org/10.1080/13527258.2018.1517374.
Shackel, Paul A. 2018c. "Transgenerational Impact of Structural Violence: Epigenetics and the Legacy of Anthracite Coal." *International Journal of Historical Archaeology* 22(4): 865–82. doi.org/10.1007/s10761-017-0451-0.
Shackel, Paul A., and Michael Roller P. 2012. "The Gilded Age Wasn't So Gilded in the Anthracite Region of Pennsylvania." *International Journal of Historical Archaeology* 16(4): 761–75.
Shackel, Paul A., and V. Camille Westmont. 2016. "When the Mines Closed: Heritage Building in Northeastern Pennsylvania." *General Anthropology* 32(1): 1–10. doi.org/10.1111/gena.12007.
Shenon, Philip. 1993. "Made in the U.S.A.? Hard Labor on a Pacific Island/ A Special Report: Saipan Sweatshops Are No American Dream." *New York Times*, 18 July. http://www.nytimes.com/1993/07/18/world/made-usa-hard-labor-pacific-island-special-report-saipan-sweatshops-are-no.html?pagewanted=all.
Shields, Mark. 1998. "'Made in the USA' Is at Heart of the Second Battle of Saipan." *Seattle Post-Intelligencer*, 18 May, A7.
Simmel, Georg. [1911] 1959. "The Ruin." In *Georg Simmel, 1858–1918: A Collection of Essays with Translations and a Bibliography*, ed. Kurt H. Wolff, 259–66. Columbus: Ohio State University Press.
Sly, Liz. 2011. "Uncharted Revolt: Act of Courage that Launched a Revolution; In Egypt, Labor's Role Largely Forgotten." *Washington Post*, 31 December, A1, A9.

Smedley, Audrey. 1998. "Race and the Construction of Human Identity." *American Anthropologist* 100(3): 690–702

Smith, Laurajane, and Gary Campbell. 2017. "'Nostalgia for the Future': Memory, Nostalgia and the Politics of Class." *International Journal of Heritage Studies* 23(7): 612–27.

Smith, Laurajane, Paul A. Shackel, and Gary Campbell, eds. 2011. *Heritage, Labour and the Working Classes*. New York: Routledge Press.

Smith, Richmond M. 1886. "American Labor Statistics." *Political Science Quarterly* 1(1): 45–83.

Smith, Richmond M. 1887. "Review: Emigration and Immigration: Reports of the Consular Offices of the United States." *Political Science Quarterly* 2(3): 520–22.

Solomon, Barbara. 1956. *Ancestors and Immigrants*. Cambridge, MA: Harvard University Press.

Sotero, Michelle M. 2006. "A Conceptual Model of Historical Trauma: Implications for Public Health Practice and Research." *Journal of Health Disparities Research and Practice* 1(1): 93–108.

Srivastava, Mehul. 2013. "Begum Losing Legs Is Bangladesh Women's Faustian Bargain." *Bloomberg News*, 5 May. https://www.bloomberg.com/news/articles/2013-05-06/begum-losing-legs-is-bangladesh-women-s-faustian-bargain.

Stanton, William. 1960. *The Leopard's Spots: Scientific Attitudes Toward Race in America, 1815–59*. Chicago: University of Chicago Press.

Steckel, Richard H., and Garrett Senney. 2015. "Historical Origins of a Major Killer: Cardiovascular Disease in the American South." Working Paper 21809. NBER Working Paper Series. National Bureau of Economic Research 1050, Cambridge, MA. http://www.nber.org/papers/w21809.

Stepenoff, Bonnie. 1999. *Their Fathers' Daughter: Silk Mill Workers in Northeastern Pennsylvania, 1880–1960*. Selinsgrove, PA: Susquehanna University Press.

Sterba, Christopher M. 1996, "Family, Work, and Nation: Hazleton, Pennsylvania and the 1934 General Strikes in Textiles." *The Pennsylvania Magazine of History and Biography* 120(1–2): 3–35.

Stevenson, George Edward. 1931. *Reflections of an Anthracite Engineer*. Scranton, PA. Self-published.

Stoler, Ann Laura. 2008. "Imperial Debris: Reflections on Ruins and Ruination." *Quarterly Anthropology* 23(2): 191–219.

Stoler, Ann Laura. 2013. "Introduction: 'The Rot Remains'; From Ruins to Ruination." In *Imperial Debris: On Ruins and Ruination*, ed. Ann Laura Stoler, 1–35. Durham, NC: Duke University Press.

Story 1. n.d. "Bound by Contract and Fear to Their Employers." Story 1. www.oddcast.com/witness/saipan.

Story 2b. n.d. "Extremely Vulnerable to Exploitation: Indentured Servitude." Story 2b. www.oddcast.com/witness/saipan.

Story 5a. n.d. "Exempt from the US Minimum Wage Law: History of the Commonwealth of the Northern Mariana Islands (CNMI)." Story 5a. www.oddcast.com/witness/saipan.

Story 6. n.d. "We Worked So Hard for Money: Lack of Monitoring." Story 6. www.oddcast.com/witness/saipan.

Strangleman, Tim. 2013. "'Smokestack Nostalgia,' 'Ruin Porn' or Working-Class Obituary: The Role and Meaning of Deindustrial Representation." *International Labor and Working-Class History* 84: 23–37.

Su, Julie. 1997. "El Monte Thai Garment Workers: Slave Sweatshops." In *No Sweat: Fashion Free Trade, and the Rights of Garment Workers*, ed. Andrew Ross, 143–49. New York: Verso.

Sudarkasa, Niara. 1968. "Racial Classifications: Popular and Scientific." *Science and the Concept of Race* 1: 149–64.

Susser, E., James Kirkbride, Bas Heijmans, Jacob Kresovich, L. H. Lumey, and Aryeh Stein. 2012. "Maternal Prenatal Nutrition and Health in Grandchildren and Subsequent Generations." *Annual Review of Anthropology* 41: 577–610.

Szymanski, Mallory. 2005. "Reflection." *News-Item* (Shamokin, PA), 25 June, C1.

Tabane, R. 2012. "Lonmin Violence: It's D-Day for the Unions." *Mail and Guardian*, 17 August. http:// mg.co.za/article/2012-08-17-00-d-day-for-the-unions.

Tarone, L. A. 2004. *We Were Here Once: Successes, Mistakes, & Calamities in Hazleton Area History*. Hazleton, PA: Citizen Publishing.

Thayer, Zaneta, and Christopher W. Kuzawa. 2011. "Biological Memories of Past Environments: Epigenetic Pathways to Health Disparities." *Epigenetics* 6 (7): 798–803.

Thomas, David Hurst. 2000. *Skull Wars: Kennewick Man, Archaeology, and the Battle for Native American Identity*. New York: Basic Books.

Thornhill, Ted. 2014. "Turkey's Prime Minister Is Accused of Punching a Mourner in the Aftermath of the Country's Worst Ever Mining Disaster." *Daily Mail*, 15 May. http://www.dailymail.co.uk/news/article-2629101/Hope-fades-150-trapped-miners-fire-STILL-burns-mile-underground-Turkish-coalmine.html.

Toisi, Niren. 2012. "Miners Killed Like 'Possessed Vermin,' Says Lawyer." *Mail & Guardian*, 22 October. https://mg.co.za/article/2012-10-22-miners-killed-like-possessed-vermin-says-lawyer.

Toksabay, Ece, and Tuvan Gumrukcu. 2018. "Turkish Court Jails Executives over 2014 Mine Disaster." Reuters, 11 July. https://www.reuters.com/article/us-turkey-mine-trial/turkish-court-jails-executives-over-2014-mine-disaster-idUSKBN1K10YI.

Turner, George A. 1977. "The Lattimer Massacre and Its Sources." *Slovakia* 27(50): 9–43.

Tuysuz, Gul, and Laura Smith-Spark. 2014. "Arrests in Deadly Turkish Mine Fire." CNN, 19 May. http://edition.cnn.com/2014/05/18/world/europe/turkey-mine-accident.

Tylor, E. B. 1871. *Primitive Culture: Research into the Development of Mythology, Philosophy, Art, and Custom.* Vols. 1 and 2. London: John Murray.

Tylor, E. B. 1881. *Anthropology: An Introduction to the Study of Man and Civilization.* London: Macmillan.

United Mine Workers Journal. 2007. "110 Years after Lattimer, Hard Coal Miners Still Fighting for Justice: The UMWA in the Anthracite." 118(5): 3–5.

US Census Bureau. 2000. "Metropolitan Area Census Data: Age & Sex." http://www.census-charts.com/Metropolitan/AgeSex.html.

US Department of Labor. 1915. *US Department of Labor, Children's Bureau, Publication 9.* Washington DC: US Government Printing Office.

US Department of Labor. 1922. *Child Labor and the Welfare of Children in an Anthracite Coal Mining District, Publication 106.* Washington DC: US Government Printing Office. https://books.google.com/books?id=Br6B6i1kcsAC.

USGS (US Geological Survey). 2017. "Coal-Mine-Drainage Projects in Pennsylvania." Pennsylvania Water Science Center. Washington DC: United States Geological Survey. https://pa.water.usgs.gov/projects/energy/amd.

US House of Representatives. 1912. 62nd Congress, 2nd Session, Committee on Immigration and Naturalization, Hearings Relative to the Further Restriction of Immigration. Washington DC: US Government Printing Office.

US Senate, 1911a. 61st Congress, 3rd Session, *Reports of the Immigration Commission*, Vol. 1, Abstracts. Washington DC: US Government Printing Office.

US Senate 1911b. 61st Congress, 3rd Session, *Reports of the Immigration Commission*, Vol. 5, *Dictionary of Races or People*. Washington DC: US Government Printing Office.

Vallejera, Jayvee L. 2007. "NMI Minimum Wage Hike OK'd." *Saipan Tribune*, 27 May. http://www.saipantribune.com/newsstory.aspx?cat=1&newsID=68875.

Vick, Karl. 2014. "Anger at Turkish Mine Disaster Rebounds on Erdogan." *Time*, 14 May. http://time.com/99675/turkey-mine-disaster-erdogan-soma.

Visweswaran, Kamala. 1998. "Race and the Culture of Anthropology." *American Anthropologist* 100(1): 70–83.

Walker, Francis A. 1891. "The Tide of Economic Thought." *Publications of the American Economic Association* 6: 15–38.

Wallace, Anthony F. C. 1987. *St. Clair: A Nineteenth-Century Coal Town's Experience with a Disaster Prone Industry.* New York: Knopf.

Washburn, Sherwood L. 1963. "The Study of Race." *American Anthropologist* 65(3): 521–31.

Washington Post. 2013. "South Africa. Panel: Police Lied About Mine Shooting." 20 September, A10.

Watson, Ivan, Gul Tuysuz, and Greg Botelho. 2014. "Despair, Anger, Dwindling Hope after Turkey Coal Mine Fire." CNN, 14 May. http://www.cnn.com/2014/05/14/world/europe/turkey-mine-accident.

Watson, Ronald R., and Victor R. Preedy, eds. 2013. *Bioactive Food as Dietary Interventions for Cardiovascular Disease.* Cambridge, MA: Academic Press.

Westmont, V. Camille. 2017. *Archaeological Investigations of Site 36LU332 House #38/40 Back Street Eckley Miners' Village, Luzerne County, Pennsylvania. Final Report*. Prepared for the Pennsylvania Historic and Museum Commission, Harrisburg, PA, by University of Maryland, Department of Anthropology, College Park, MD.

Westmont, V. Camille. 2019. "Creating Anthracite Women: The Role of Architecture and Material Culture in Identity Formation in Pennsylvania Anthracite Company Towns, 1854–1940." PhD dissertation. College Park, MD: Department of Anthropology, University of Maryland.

White, Gillian B. 2015. "Are Factories in Bangladesh Any Safer Now?" *Atlantic*, 17 December. https://www.theatlantic.com/business/archive/2015/12/bangladesh-factory-workers/421005.

Wiebe, Robert H. 1961. "The Anthracite Coal Strike of 1902: A Record of Confusion." *Mississippi Valley Historical Review* 48(2): 229–51.

Wolensky, Kenneth C. 2003. "An Industry on Wheels." In *Sweatshop USA: The American Sweatshop in Historical and Global Perspective*, ed. Daniel Bender and Richard Greenwald, 91–116. New York: Routledge.

Wolensky, Robert P., and Joseph M. Keating. 2008. *Tragedy at Avondale: The Causes, Consequences, and Legacy of the Pennsylvania Anthracite Coal Industry's Most Deadly Mining Disaster, September 6, 1869*. Easton, PA: Canal History and Technology Press.

Wolensky, Robert P., Nicole H. Wolensky, and Kenneth C. Wolensky. 2005. *Voices of the Knox Mine Disaster: Stories, Remembrances, and Reflections of the Anthracite Coal Industry's Last Major Catastrophe, January 22, 1959*. Harrisburg: Pennsylvania Historical and Museum Commission.

Wolff, Richard D. 2013. "Economic Development and Rana Plaza." *Monthly Review*, 16 May. https://mronline.org/2013/05/16/wolff160513-html.

Woman's Institute of Domestic Arts and Sciences. 1923. *Woman's Institute Library of Cookery*. Scranton, PA: Woman's Institute of Domestic Arts and Sciences.

Wyoming Valley Women's Club. 1925. *Wyoming Valley Women's Club Cook Book*. Wilkes-Barre, PA: Caxton Press.

Wysocki, Bernard, Jr. 1978. "Review of *The Guns of Lattimer*, by Michael Novak." *Wall Street Journal*, 13 December, 24.

Yardley, Jim 2013a. "After Bangladesh Factory Collapse, Bleak Struggle for Survivors." *New York Times*, 18 December. http://www.nytimes.com/2013/12/19/world/asia/after-collapse-bleak-struggle.html?pagewanted=all.

Yardley, Jim. 2013b. "Last Hope in Ruins: Bangladesh's Race to Save Shaheena." *New York Times*, 5 May. http://www.nytimes.com/2013/05/06/world/asia/struggle-in-bangladesh-to-save-collapse-survivor.html.

Ydstie, John. 2006. "The Abramoff-DeLay-Mariana Islands Connection: Six Degrees of Jack Abramoff." *NPR*, 17 June. http://www.npr.org/templates/story/story.php?storyId=5492833.

Yeginsu, Ceylan. 2015. "Anger and Grief Simmer in Turkey a Year after Soma Mine Disaster." *New York Times*, 2 June. https://www.nytimes.com/2015/06/03/world/europe/anger-and-grief-simmer-in-turkey-a-year-after-soma-mine-disaster.html.

Yellen, Samuel. 1936. *American Labor Struggles*. New York: S. A. Russell.

Zawacki, Gabby. 2015. "Abandoned Mine Drainage: Past Causes and Present Impacts." Anthracite Environmental, 12 June. https://anthraciteenvironmental.org/2015/06/12/abandoned-mine-drainage/

Zinn, Howard. 2003. *A People's History of the United States: 1492–Present*. New York: HarperCollins.

INDEX

acid mine drainage (AMD), 53–55
acid rock drainage (ARD), 54
Amalgamated Association of Mines and Mine Laborers, 19
Amalgamated Clothing and Textile Workers Union, 78
American Federation of Labor (AFL), 28, 74, 92
American School (of evolutionary theory), 15
Anthracite Coal Strike Commission, 22–23
Anthracite Coal Strike of 1900, 20–21, 92
Anthracite Coal Strike of 1902, The Great, 21–23, 74, 92
Anthracite Heritage Projects, ix, x, 29, 61
archaeology, 3–5, 8–9, 11, 29, 59, 70. *See also under* Lattimer No. 2
Association of Mineworkers and Construction Union (AMCU), 93, 96
Avondale mine disaster, 1

Bangladesh. *See under* textile industry
Battlefield Restoration and Archaeological Volunteer Organization (BRAVO), ix
Bench Marks Foundation, 98–99
Blaschak Coal Company, 59

Campbell Act (1897), 2
carbon sequestration, 57
Centers for Disease Control and Prevention, 9, 63–68
Centralia, 70, 111
child labor, 32, 74
class. *See under* heritage
Coal and Iron Police, 2, 33
Coal Mine Safety Act of 1969, 92
commemoration, 109–111
Commonwealth of the Northern Mariana Islands (CNMI), 10, 77–82, 115
  Covenant to Establish the Commonwealth of the Northern Mariana Islands in Political Union with the United States, 77–78
  immigration to, 78, 81
  labor laws in, 78–82
counter memory, 110
creative destruction, 111–112

deindustrialization. *See under* Northeastern Pennsylvania
Dhaka. *See under* textile industry
Duplan Silk Complex, 73–76

Earth Conservancy, 53, 55–56
Eckley Miners' Village, ix, 59–60
El Monte factory, 114
epigenetics, 65–71

eugenics, 8, 38
Evangelical Alliance, 38

Gallup, 9, 63
gardens, 40–43, 49. *See also under* Slavic
Great Depression, 40, 42, 47
Great Famine, 13

Haymarket, 2
Hazle Realty Company, 40, 42, 47
Hazleton, Pennsylvania, 2, 8, 13, 19, 21, 38, 40, 45, 56, 63, 64, 68, 73–77, 113
Hazleton strike, 19
heritage, ix, x, 4–7, 10, 29, 61, 85, 90, 110, 113, 116
    class, 117–120
    social justice and, 4, 7, 11, 90, 117–119
historic trauma, 50–71, 113
Historical Collections and Labor Archives (*HCLA*), ix
homestead, 2

Immigration Commission, 8, 23–25, 27, 38
Immigration Restriction League (IRL), 17–18, 23, 28
Industrial Commission of Transportation, 19
industrial landscape. 7, 11
Industrial Revolution, 1, 12, 94
integrated gasification combined cycle (IGCC) technology, 57
International Labor Organization, 87–88, 101, 102, 106
International Ladies' Garment Workers' Union (ILGWU), 10, 72, 78
International Workers of the World (IWW), 6, 22, 74–75

Keystone Opportunity Zone, 113
Knights of Labor, 19, 34

landscape
    environmental impact on, 51–59
    ruined, 110–111
Lattimer Coal Company, 37, 40, 42, 48
Lattimer massacre (1897), 4, 6, 10, 19, 73, 92–93, 116
    commemorative events related to, 7
    Roman Catholic Church connection to, 7
Lattimer Mines. *See under* Lattimer No. 1
Lattimer No. 1, 36, 39, 60
    Lattimer Mines, 2, 36, 38, 60
Lattimer No. 2, ix, 36–50
    archaeology at, 36–41
    Italian village in, 36–41
    Pardeesville, ix
    sanitation in, 45–48
Lonmin's Marikana Platinum Mine. *See under* mining
Ludlow, 2

Marikana massacre, 93–99
    memorialization of, 99–100
Massey Energy, 101, 116–117
Mine Safety and Health Administration (MSHA), 58, 92, 117
mining
    Anglo American Platinum, 96
    Lonmin's Marikana Platinum Mine, South Africa, 10, 93–100
    Soma, Turkey and, 100–109
    United States and, ix, 1–3, 6–9, 12, 19, 23, 32–345, 45, 46, 51–53, 55–58, 67–69, 75, 91–93
monogenist, 14–15

National Union Mineworkers (NUM), 93
nativism, 8, 17

Northeastern Pennsylvania, 12–14
   deindustrialization of, 52,
      72–77, 111–112
   historic living conditions, 32–36
   structural violence in, 50–51
   subsidence, 56–57, 69
   unhappiest place, 63–64
Northern Italian(s), 17, 24, 25, 38

Pardeesville, viii, ix, 36–47. *See also under* Lattimer No. 2
Patriotic Order Sons of America, 24
Paterson strike, 74–75
polygenism, 15–16

race, 14–18
   employment and, 18–21
   structural violence and, 18
   Slavic immigration and, 29–31
   housing and, 33–36
Rana Plaza. *See under* textile industry
Red Scare, 6
Reports of the Immigration Commission (1911), 8, 23–25, 27, 38
ruination, 112–113
rust belt, 63

scientific racism, 8, 14, 16, 25–27
Scranton, Pennsylvania, 5, 7, 13, 32, 61, 63, 64, 68, 74
Slavic, 13, 24
   gardens, 43–46
   infant mortality rate among, 32
   living conditions among, 32–33
   immigration of, 29–31
   living conditions of, 32–33
social justice. *See under* heritage
Soma, Turkey mine disaster, 10, 100–109, 116–119
Southern Italian(s), 17, 18, 24, 25, 38

St. Nazarius, 37–39
structural violence, 9, 18, 49, 62, 64, 111, 113. *See also under* Northeastern Pennsylvania
subsidence. *See under* Northeastern Pennsylvania
supermodernity, 5
sweatshops, 11, 76, 114–115

Tazreen Fashion Factory. *See under* textile industry
Testimony to Investigating Committee, U.S. House of Representatives, 34
textile industry
   Bangladesh and, 8, 79, 82–89, 115–116, 119
   Commonwealth of Northern Mariana Islands and, 77–82
   Dhaka, 83, 84, 85–86, 119
   Northeastern Pennsylvania and, 72–77
   Rana Plaza, 83–89, 116
   Tazreen Fashion Factory, 84, 86–87
   Triangle Shirtwaist Factory fire of 1911, 83
Triangle Shirtwaist Factory fire of 1911. *See under* textile industry

United Mine Workers of America (UMWA), 2, 19–23, 28, 92
United Nations Educational, Scientific, and Cultural Organization (UNESCO), 27
United Textile Workers of America (UTWA), 74–75
Universal Races Congress, 26

Wilkes-Barre, 12, 13, 22, 56, 61–64, 68

www.ingramcontent.com/pod-product-compliance
Lightning Source LLC
Chambersburg PA
CBHW071714020426
42333CB00017B/2260